The Roaring Twenties and Great Depression

Author:	Cindy Barden
Editor:	Mary Dieterich
Contributor:	Karl Mechem
Proofreaders:	Alexis Fey and April Hawkins

COPYRIGHT © 2025 Mark Twain Media, Inc.

ISBN 978-1-62223-905-4

Printing No. CD-405091

Mark Twain Media, Inc., Publishers
Distributed by Carson Dellosa Education

Table of Contents

Introduction to the Teacher

Welcome to *The Roaring Twenties and Great Depression,* one of the books in the Mark Twain Media, Inc., American History series for students in grades 5–8+.

The activity books in this series are designed as stand-alone material for classrooms and home-schoolers or as supplemental material to enhance your history curriculum. Students can be encouraged to use the books as independent study units to improve their understanding of historical events and people.

This book provides challenging activities that enable students to explore history, geography, and social studies topics associated with the Roaring Twenties and the Great Depression. The activities provide research opportunities and promote critical reading, thinking, and writing skills. As students learn about the people and events that influenced history, they will draw conclusions; write opinions; compare and contrast historical events, people, and places; analyze cause and effect; and improve mapping and thinking skills. Students will also have the opportunity to apply what they learn to their own lives through reflection and creative writing.

Students can further increase their knowledge and understanding of these historical events by using reference sources at the library and on the Internet. Students may need assistance to discover appropriate websites.

Titles of books for additional reading appropriate to the subject matter at this grade level are included at the end of the book.

Although many of the questions are open-ended, answer keys are included at the back of the book for questions with specific answers.

Listening to the radio in the mid 1920s

Timeline of the Roaring Twenties: 1920–1929

1913–1921	U.S. President: Woodrow Wilson
1919	The Eighteenth Amendment prohibits the sale of liquor.
1920	U.S. census = 105,710,620 people The Nineteenth Amendment grants women the right to vote. The first U.S. cross-country airmail flight is completed. The average life expectancy in the United States is 54.09 years.
1921–1923	U.S. President: Warren G. Harding
1921	The first skywriting takes place.
1922	The *Reader's Digest* magazine is first published. The first experimental car radios are developed.
1923–1929	U.S. President: Calvin Coolidge
1923	Neon signs are introduced. A.C. Nielson begins measuring radio audiences. A speech by President Harding is broadcast on the radio. *Time* magazine is first published.
1924	The first Disney cartoon, "Alice's Wonderland," is produced. The first perms for hair are available. The Teapot Dome Scandal becomes public. The Model T Ford is sold for $290.
1925	The Goodyear blimp begins sky advertising. *The New Yorker* magazine is first published. The "Grand Ole Opry" radio show begins in Nashville. Warner Brothers begins experimenting with "talkies" (movies with sound).
1926	The Book-of-the-Month Club begins. The first radio jingle is broadcast (Wheaties™). NBC is formed. Zippers become available.
1927	CBS is formed. The Holland Tunnel is opened.
1928	The first teletype machine is used. The first Disney cartoon with sound, "Steamboat Willie," is produced. The first television sets in the United States are installed in three homes.
1929	The first Academy Awards are presented. Experiments begin with color television. The stock market crashes; the Great Depression begins.

Timeline of the Great Depression: 1929–1939

1929–1933   U.S. President: Herbert Hoover
1930   U.S. census = 122,775,046 people
   "Blondie and Dagwood" becomes a daily comic strip.
   The National Unemployed Council is formed.
1931   Commercial teletype service begins.
   "The Star-Spangled Banner" becomes the national anthem.
   The Empire State Building is opened.
   The Davis-Bacon Act provides for the payment of prevailing wages to workers
      employed on public works projects.
1932   The Lindbergh baby is kidnapped.
   The first Winter Olympics held in the United States are held at Lake Placid, NY.
   Unemployment reaches 13,000,000.
   The Norris-LaGuardia Act prohibits federal injunctions in labor disputes.
   The cost of mailing a letter rises from two cents to three cents.
1933–1945   U.S. President: Franklin D. Roosevelt
1933   Franklin D. Roosevelt begins radio "Fireside Chats."
   The first real comic book is published: *Funnies on Parade.*
   The Twenty-First Amendment repeals Prohibition.
   The National Industrial Recovery Act guarantees the rights of employees to organize
      and bargain collectively.
   Frances Perkins becomes Secretary of Labor (first woman named to a presidential
      Cabinet).
   The first drive-in movie theater opens (Camden, NJ).
   Minimum wage is set at 40 cents an hour.
1934   "High-fidelity" records become available.
   One-half of the homes in the United States have radios.
1935   IBM begins selling electric typewriters.
   The Social Security Act is signed.
1936   The BBC begins the world's first television service, three hours a day.
   The electric guitar is invented.
   LIFE, the magazine, is first published.
1937   The electrical digital calculator is invented.
   A child labor law is passed.
   Nylon is invented.
   Look magazine is first published.
   The Golden Gate Bridge opens.
1938   Disney produces its first full-length animated film, *Snow White and the Seven Dwarfs.*
   The Fair Labor Standards Act establishes the 40-hour work week, the minimum
      wage, and bans child labor in interstate commerce.
   Superman was "born."
1939   Television is demonstrated at the New York World's Fair.
   World War II begins in Europe.

Name: _______________________________________ Date: _____________________________

The Decade That Roared

The 1920s was one of the wildest periods in American history. When World War I ended in 1919, Americans looked to the new decade with hope for world peace. The inventions and advancements developed during the war could now be put to peaceful uses. Society rejoiced; people abandoned traditions. New rules were made—and broken.

The Eighteenth Amendment to the Constitution in 1919 made it illegal to import, sell, or manufacture alcoholic beverages—a law that was broken at every level of society.

Rapid advancements in communications, transportation, and technology caused people to coin a new phrase: "What will they think of next?"

Electricity was so new that many people were afraid of it. They bought special caps to put over electrical outlets so the electricity wouldn't spill out into the room. In 1919, only about one-third of American homes had electricity. That number had doubled by 1929.

Electricity reached many more homes during the 1920s.

With the introduction of the assembly line, car manufacturers began producing great numbers of automobiles at a much lower cost. In 1924, people could buy a brand new Ford Model T for $290. Over 23,000,000 cars jammed American roads by 1929.

At the beginning of the decade, movies were black and white and had no sound. Warner Brothers introduced the first color film, complete with sound, in 1929.

Passage of the Nineteenth Amendment granting women the right to vote ushered in a new era of women's rights. Women also enjoyed more freedom in their personal lives, wearing new hairstyles and daring dresses so short, they showed their knees in public!

People were anxious to put thoughts of war behind them and enjoy life with a vigor never seen before. Although the decade began on a high note, it ended with fear of economic ruin. The good times came to an end with the Stock Market Crash of 1929.

1. List ten items in your home that wouldn't work without electricity.

____

____

____

2. Of those items, which would you miss most? Why?

____

____

____

____

Name: ____ Date: _________________________

Prohibition Becomes the Law

For decades, many **temperance** groups—led mainly by women and various religious organizations—had tried to make alcohol illegal in the United States. Some blamed alcohol for the rising rates in divorce, family problems, crimes, violence, and poverty. Others felt the grain used to make alcohol could be better used for food.

By 1916, 23 of the 48 states had passed anti-saloon laws that closed taverns and prohibited the manufacture of intoxicating beverages. In 1919, the Eighteenth Amendment to the U.S. Constitution made the manufacture, sale, import, or export of liquor illegal anywhere in the United States.

Agents pour illegal liquor into the sewer during Prohibition.

The Eighteenth Amendment did not make it illegal to possess liquor or to drink it. Exceptions were also made for liquor sold for medicinal, sacramental, and industrial purposes. It also excluded fruit and grape beverages prepared for personal use at home.

Congress passed the Volstead Act to enforce Prohibition, but the government had too little money and too few personnel to be effective.

Even though all taverns and saloons were officially closed, illegal taverns and nightclubs—called **speakeasies**—sprang up everywhere. People smuggled liquor across the border from Canada, imported it illegally from Europe and the Caribbean Islands, and produced it in illegal factories. Prohibition gave criminals a wonderful opportunity to grow rich by providing "**bootleg**" alcohol.

1. What is your opinion of the use of alcoholic beverages? Does it cause problems?

   ____

   ____

2. Why do you think some exceptions were made to the Prohibition law?

   ____

   ____

3. Why do you think Prohibition was called "the Noble Experiment"?

   ____

   ____

4. Do you think the government has the right to ban alcohol, tobacco, drugs, or any other product? Why or why not?

   ____

   ____

Name: _________________________________ Date: _________________________

Warren G. Harding's Presidency

Born: November 2, 1865
Term of office: March 4, 1921–August 2, 1923
Occupation: Newspaper publisher
Political Party: Republican

Warren G. Harding

When World War I finally ended, Warren Harding believed the country needed a "return to normalcy," which became his campaign slogan.

Harding stressed Americanism and offered hope to people tired of war. He arranged a peace treaty signed with Germany in 1921. With Charles G. Dawes as director, the national budget was cut from six billion to three billion dollars, and at the end of 1922, there was even a surplus.

Rumors of scandal, corruption, and dishonest deals at high levels in the government began in 1922. Although Harding himself was not accused of wrongdoing, his administration is remembered for its corruption.

Charles R. Forbes, head of the Veterans Bureau and a personal friend of Harding's, was tried for bribery and conspiracy. He had authorized hundreds of millions of dollars for overpriced materials, sites, and construction.

Secretary of the Interior Albert Fall was convicted of accepting an illegal payment of $400,000 in return for turning over two valuable tracts of land to private oil companies.

Attorney General Harry Daugherty, another close friend of Harding's, stood trial twice for conspiring to defraud the government by selling government favors. Both times the juries were unable to reach a verdict, and the case was finally dropped.

1. What do you think Harding meant by a "return to normalcy"?

   ____

   ____

   ____

2. How do you think Harding felt when he learned that some of his closest friends were accused of corruption and fraud?

   ____

   ____

3. Since Harding personally appointed these men to their positions, do you think he was partly to blame for their actions? Why or why not?

   ____

   ____

   ____

Name: _______________________________ Date: _______________________________

Women Finally Allowed to Vote

Nineteenth Amendment

The right of citizens of the United States to vote shall not be denied or abridged by the United States or any state on account of sex.

The campaign for women's **suffrage** (the right to vote) began in the 1840s, long before the Nineteenth Amendment was finally ratified in 1920. Many states had granted women full or partial suffrage before 1920. The election of 1920 was the first time all women were allowed to vote for the president.

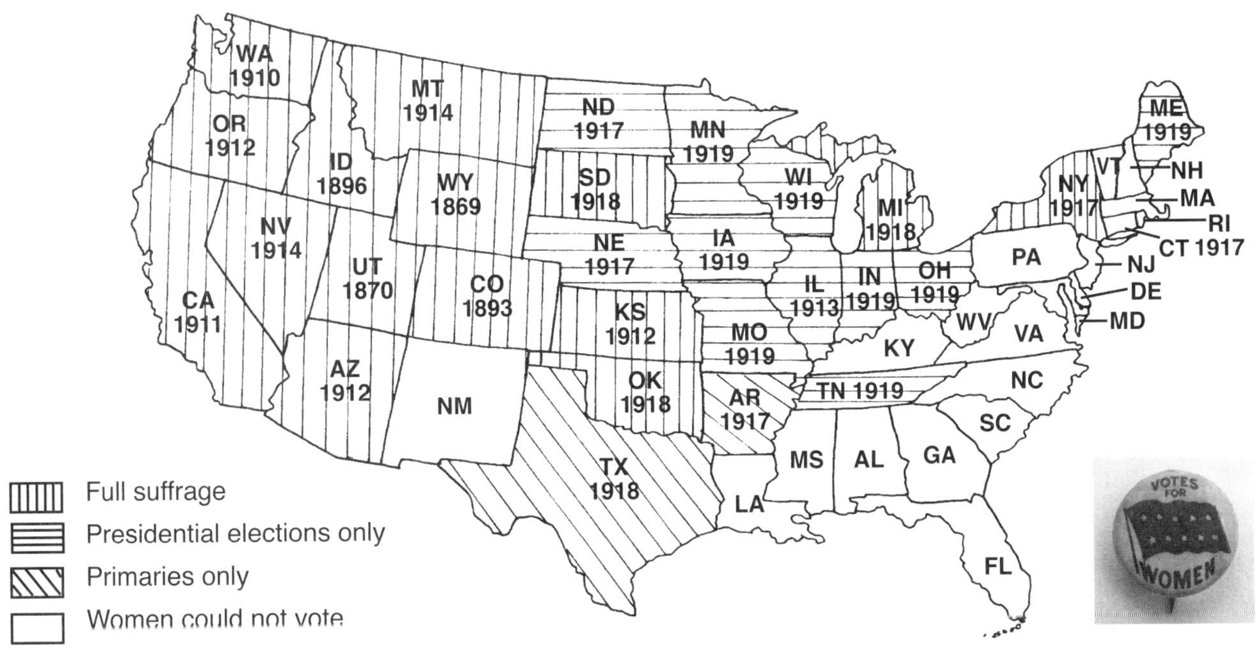

1. Which state was the first to grant full suffrage to women? _______________________

2. List five states that did not allow women the right to vote before the Nineteenth Amendment was passed.

    ____

3. List five states that allowed women to vote in all elections before the Nineteenth Amendment was passed.

    ____

4. Geographically, what stands out about states that had granted women the right to vote before the Nineteenth Amendment was passed and those that hadn't?

    ____

    ____

Name: _________________________________ Date: _________________________________

Flaming Youth

Actress Alice Joyce wearing a
flapper-style dress and hairdo

A social revolution took place among young people during the twenties. Nicknamed the "Flaming Youth," they lived for pleasure, enjoyed fast-paced music and vigorous dances, wore "scandalous" fashions and hairdos, and developed a taste for zany stunts like flagpole sitting and marathon dances.

Young women called "**flappers**" began dressing in ways that outraged their parents. Previously, women's dresses had covered them completely from neck to ankles. Suddenly, fashions changed. Necklines plunged, and hemlines rose above the knees.

Young women defied authority by wearing makeup, smoking cigarettes, and cutting their hair short.

In Utah, lawmakers tried to make it illegal for women to wear "skirts higher than three inches above the ankle."

Marathons became the craze in the twenties. Dance marathons went on nonstop for days. The last couple standing won a prize. Other marathon events included kissing contests, roller-skating, and flagpole sitting.

1. If you had been a parent then, how do you think you would have felt about your daughter wearing the new styles of clothing?

____

____

2. If you had been a young person then, how do you think you would have felt about twenties' fashions?

____

____

3. What current fashion in clothing, jewelry, or hairstyle do your parents dislike?

____

4. How do you feel about it? ____

____

5. Do you think any government has the right to regulate what people wear? Why or why not?

____

____

Name: _________________________________   Date: _________________________

Americans on the Go

Model T

Henry Ford built his first car in 1896. By 1908, the Ford Motor Company had produced a simple, reliable car called the Model T. Nicknamed the Tin Lizzie, its 20-horsepower engine allowed drivers to reach a top speed of 40 miles per hour.

Early Fords cost $850—a very high price for the times. At first, cars were considered "toys" only the very rich could afford. That changed when Ford introduced an efficient assembly line for production. The price of a new Ford dropped to $290 in 1924.

The Ford Motor Company described the Model T as "an inexpensive vehicle for the great multitude." People could buy cars on the installment plan.

In 1927, the Ford Motor Company discontinued making the Model T and replaced it with the more modern Model A, which sold for $395. Henry Ford announced, "Any customer can have a car painted any color that he wants so long as it is black."

Model A

Even at under $300 dollars, owning a car usually meant either saving for a long time or buying on credit. Most women did not have jobs outside the home. Men working at good jobs in the auto industry made between $5 and $7 per day and worked six-day weeks during the 1920s, though most jobs paid much less.

1. List three ways owning a car might have affected a 1920s family that had never owned a car before.

   ____

   ____

   ____

2. Ford Motor Company was not the only important car manufacturer in the United States during the 1920s. Use reference sources to find the names of three other major car makers during that time period.

   ____

   ____

3. Imagine being a child in the mid-1920s. You want to convince your parents it would be a good idea to buy an automobile. On your own paper, give three good reasons.

Name: _________________________________   Date: _______________________

Automobiles Change America

Mass production of automobiles affected both society and the economy. As more people bought cars, more jobs were created in the auto industry, and wages rose. The demand for cars also created more jobs in industries that made steel, glass, rubber, petroleum, and other products used to build cars.

In a widely reported interview of the time, a farm wife was asked why her family owned a car but not a bathtub. "You can't go to town in a bathtub," she replied.

As more people drove cars, the roads became very crowded. People demanded a better road system with improved roads. In 1909, the United States had only 750 miles of paved roads. By 1930, that number had risen to more than 100,000 miles.

Road construction provided jobs for crews and suppliers of materials. As more roads were built, people traveled more. Along the new roads, businesses like gas stations, diners, hot dog stands, and tourist cabins grew to meet the demand of travelers.

Car dealers and used car lots were seen for the first time. The first modern gas stations opened in 1913. By 1929, the country had 121,500 gas stations (an average of more than one per mile of paved road).

Not only did automobile companies make cars, they also built millions of taxis, buses, and trucks. Between 1904 and 1929, the number of trucks registered in the United States rose from 700 to 3.4 million.

1. List three types of businesses today that wouldn't exist if people didn't have cars.

    ____

    ____

2. What businesses might have been affected when trucks and buses replaced stagecoaches and horse-drawn wagons?

    ____

    ____

    ____

3. Draw a cartoon about what the farm wife above might have said about any other aspect of owning a car in the 1920s.

Name: _________________________________ Date: _________________________

Welcome to the Jazz Age

Jazz is a uniquely American style of music that evolved from spirituals, blues, and ragtime. Jazz first burst forth in the early 1900s in New Orleans. At first, jazz featured enthusiasm, volume, and improvisation rather than finesse. Early jazz was performed mainly by small marching bands or solo pianists and became popular at weddings, picnics, parades, and funerals.

King & Carter Jazzing Orchestra in 1921

Although jazz developed among Black musicians, no sound recordings remain of the earliest jazz groups. The first surviving jazz recording, made in 1917, was by an all-White group who called themselves the Original Dixieland Jazz Band. Eventually New Orleans style jazz as played by Whites came to be called Dixieland Jazz.

Jazz in the 1920s involved great experimentation and discovery. For the first time, bands began featuring soloists on trumpet, saxophone, and piano. Mamie Smith had a sudden hit in 1920 with her recording of "Crazy Blues." One of the greatest jazz singers of the twenties was Bessie Smith.

Many New Orleans jazz musicians, including Louis Armstrong and Jelly Roll Morton, became famous by performing in Chicago nightclubs. Eventually a Chicago style of jazz evolved, derived from the New Orleans style, but with more emphasis on soloists and often featuring saxophones, pianos, and vocalists. Chicago jazz had tenser rhythms and more complicated textures.

Throughout the 1920s and into the 1930s, jazz continued to be a very popular form of music.

Listen to recordings made prior to 1940 of several jazz performers or groups. Samples can be found on the Internet and at your local library.

1. Which groups did you listen to? ____

____

2. Which was your favorite group? Why? _____________________________________

____

3. If your favorite group featured a soloist, what was his/her name? _____________

____

4. Which song did you like best? ____

5. How do you feel when you listen to jazz? __________________________________

____

6. What is your opinion of jazz? ____

____

Name: _______________________________________ Date: _______________________________________

Louis Armstrong: Master of Improvisation

Born around 1901 in New Orleans, Louis Armstrong spent his first 12 years in a very poor home. His father had deserted the family. They seldom had enough to eat or decent clothing, and Louis dropped out of school after fifth grade.

When he was about 13, Louis was sent to the Colored Waifs' Home where he joined a boys' brass band. With Louis' natural ability for music as a cornet player, he soon became the star of the group. After he left the home, he played in rough clubs and dance halls in the urban slum districts of New Orleans. He couldn't afford his own cornet and had to borrow one to perform.

Louis became friends with King Oliver, a famous Black musician. After becoming part of Kid Ory's band, his reputation grew. In 1922, Louis joined Oliver's Creole Jazz Band in Chicago.

Two years later, he joined a band in New York where he dazzled both musicians and audiences with his unique loose, springy swing style and his ability to improvise.

Previously, most jazz was played by ensembles. Rarely was any one person featured for other than a short solo. Back in Chicago in 1925, Louis led his own band and began making records playing New Orleans-style jazz. The popularity of his short solos soon convinced record companies that he should be featured, with other players merely providing backup.

At first, his records featured Louis playing the trumpet. Then he began singing in a distinctive, rough voice that attracted listeners. His hit songs included "Savoy Blues," "Hotter Than That," "West End Blues," "Blueberry Hill," "Mack the Knife," "Hello, Dolly," and "What a Wonderful World."

Raised in poverty, Louis Armstrong became famous worldwide as a jazz trumpet player and singer. By the 1950s, Louis Armstrong had performed all over the world and was the most famous jazz musician of the time.

1. Use a dictionary. What does *improvise* mean? _______________________________________

   ____

2. Use a dictionary. What does *ensemble* mean? _______________________________________

   ____

Use reference sources to find the answers.

3. One of Louis Armstrong's songs hit number one on the charts in 1964. What was the name of the song?

   ____

4. What was Louis Armstrong's nickname? _______________________________________

Name: _________________________________   Date: _______________________________

Meet John Calvin Coolidge

As governor of Massachusetts, Calvin Coolidge attracted national attention when he called out the National Guard in response to a strike by the Boston police.

"There is no right to strike against the public safety by anybody, anywhere, anytime," he said.

Calvin Coolidge decided not to run for another term as president in 1928. When asked why, he replied, "Because there's no chance for advancement."

1. Do you agree or disagree? Why?

   ____

   ____

   ____

   ____

Coolidge was elected vice president under President Harding in 1920. When the president died on August 2, 1923, Coolidge became president. His first challenge was to clean up the corruption that had occurred while Harding was president.

Farmers in the western part of the country did not enjoy the prosperity of the 1920s. They wanted government aid, but Coolidge refused. Congress approved the McNary-Haugen Farm Relief Bill, which proposed that the government buy surplus crops and sell them abroad to raise domestic agricultural prices. Coolidge vetoed the bill in 1927 and again in 1928 because he felt the government had no business fixing prices.

Throughout his term as president, Coolidge retained very conservative policies. He opposed government intervention in private business.

2. Coolidge believed that the government should not interfere with private business. Do you agree or disagree? Why?

   ____

   ____

   ____

Use reference sources to answer these questions about President Coolidge.

3. When and where was he born? ____

4. What was his nickname? ____

5. What political party did he belong to? ____

6. What was his occupation before going into politics? ____________________________

7. What was his campaign slogan in the 1924 presidential election? __________________

   ____

Name: _______________________________ Date: _______________________________

At the Movies

If you had gone to a movie in 1925, it would probably have cost a dime. The movie would have been short, in black and white, and silent. In some theaters, piano players provided background music to match the action on the screen.

Charlie Chaplin (left) and Jackie Coogan (right) in the 1921 movie The Kid.

The motion-picture industry flourished in the 1920s as advances were made in filmmaking. Writers, directors, actors, and actresses moved to sunny southern California to make movies.

Mary Pickford and Charlie Chaplin, two of the most popular movie stars of the 1920s, received huge salaries— over $500,000 a year. Other favorites included Rudolph Valentino, John Gilbert, Douglas Fairbanks, Pola Negri, Gloria Swanson, and Greta Garbo.

What types of movies did people enjoy in the 1920s and 1930s? Stars like Broncho Billy, Tom Mix, and William S. Hart made Western films very popular. People enjoyed movies about crimes, like *The Great Train Robbery.* Comedies featured Charlie Chaplin, "Fatty" Arbuckle, and the *Keystone Cops.* Actresses like Theda Bara made love stories popular. Sentimental stories about children and/or animals were always a hit.

Although the stars have changed and movies are now in color with sound and plenty of special effects, current movies fit into many of the same categories that were popular in the 1920s and 1930s.

1. Making movies provided jobs for many types of people besides directors, writers, actors, and actresses. What other types of jobs are needed to make movies?

   ____

   ____

   ____

2. List a title of a modern movie for each theme.

   A Western ____

   A crime story ____

   A comedy ____

   A love story ____

   A sentimental story ____

3. What other types of movies are popular today? _______________________________

   ____

Name: _________________________________ Date: _______________________

Roaring Twenties Trivia

- In 1920, less than 15 percent of the people in the United States had a telephone.

- The National Negro Baseball League was organized on February 13, 1920.

- WEW in St. Louis, Missouri, aired the first weather news heard on radio in 1921.

- The Lincoln Memorial was dedicated in Washington, D.C., on May 30, 1922.

- Henry Berliner made the first helicopter flight on June 16, 1922, at College Park, Maryland.

- Yankee Stadium opened on April 18, 1923, in the Bronx. As the hometown team, the New York Yankees hosted the Boston Red Sox. A record crowd of 74,000 fans saw the action at the first three-level stadium in the country.

- Henry Sullivan became the first American to swim across the English Channel on August 5, 1923.

- Simon and Schuster, Inc., published the first "Crossword Puzzle Book" in April 1924.

- The presidential inauguration was broadcast on radio for the very first time when Calvin Coolidge took the oath of office in Washington, D.C., in March 1925.

- Gertrude Ederle, age 19, became the first American woman to swim the English Channel on August 26, 1926. She did it in a record-breaking time of 14 hours and 31 minutes.

- The Flatheads Gang committed the first armored car robbery near Pittsburgh, Pennsylvania, stealing $104,250 on March 11, 1927.

- Morris S. Frank received Buddy, the first seeing-eye dog, on April 25, 1928.

Use reference sources to write two other interesting bits of Roaring Twenties trivia.

1. ____

____

____

2. ____

____

____

Name: _________________________________   Date: _________________________________

What Could You Buy for a Dollar?

During the 1920s, a dollar went a long way. However, most kids only received about ten cents a week for allowance, so it took a long time to save a dollar.

1. You have one dollar to spend. If you bought a set of building blocks and went to a movie, how many pieces of penny candy could you also buy? _______________________

2. If you bought a board game and five candy bars, would you have enough change left from a dollar to go to a movie? _______________________

3. How many ice cream cones could you buy with a dollar? _______________________

4. How many weeks would you have to save your allowance (10 cents a week) to buy a sled?

    ____

5. You and three friends take the streetcar to the movie. You each have an ice cream bar as you walk home. How much did you and your friends spend in all? _______________________

Name: ____ Date: _____________________________

Learning a New Language: Twenties' Slang

Many slang words and phrases came into common use in the 1920s. As with most generations, the young people of the 1920s came up with their own codewords and phrases to describe common traits or actions.

If you thought someone was handing you a line of nonsense, you might tell them to stop the banana oil.

You could compliment a woman by telling her she was the eel's ankles, the bee's knees, or the cat's meow.

A stylish young man might be called a sheik. But beware if someone says you're a flat tire, because they think you're a boring person.

Match these 1920s terms with their definitions. Feel free to use a dictionary, the Internet, or other resources to find the answers.

_____ 1. speakeasy	A. woman's short haircut	
_____ 2. bootleg	B. an illegal tavern or nightclub	
_____ 3. guff	C. dressed up; looking good	
_____ 4. half-pint	D. posh; elegant	
_____ 5. hep	E. being lazy	
_____ 6. flapper	F. a child	
_____ 7. bob	G. tease	
_____ 8. razz	H. back talk	
_____ 9. smackeroo	I. wool pajamas with feet	
_____ 10. spiffy	J. just great	
_____ 11. two bits	K. feet	
_____ 12. horsefeathers	L. with it; up-to-date	
_____ 13. lollygagging	M. illegal	
_____ 14. mob	N. a dollar	
_____ 15. ritzy	O. a quarter	
_____ 16. dogs	P. gangsters	
_____ 17. Dr. Dentons	Q. nonsense	
_____ 18. the berries	R. stylish young woman	

Name: _______________________________________ Date: _______________________________

Twenties Scavenger Hunt

To complete this scavenger hunt, use the Internet and other reference sources to find the answers.

J.E. Clair, owner of the Acme Packing Company, bought a pro football franchise on August 27, 1921. He named the team in honor of the workers at his meat processing plant.

1. What did he name the team? ____

The first Miss America pageant was held in 1921.

2. Who was the winner? ____

The National Football League franchise in Decatur, Illinois, was transferred to another city in Illinois in January 1922.

3. What team did they become? ____

In April 1923, the Firestone Tire and Rubber Company of Akron, Ohio, began the first regular production of a new product.

4. What was the product? ____

Rin Tin Tin became a famous movie star in 1923.

5. What was Rin Tin Tin? ____

The first woman to become a state governor took office in Wyoming on January 5, 1925.

6. What was her name? ____

The first Black American basketball team was organized in 1927.

7. What was the name of the team? ____

Charles Lindbergh took off from Roosevelt Field in New York on May 20, 1927, in a small airplane. He flew nonstop to Paris, France.

8. What was the name of his plane?

____

9. How long did the flight last?

____

Penicillin was discovered in 1928.

10. Who discovered it?

____

Name: _________________________________ Date: _______________________________

Up, Up, and Away

In 1903, the Wright brothers successfully flew an airplane for the first time. They didn't fly very far, very high, or for very long—but they did fly.

Early planes were not too reliable and were considered more of a curiosity than a future means of transportation. During World War I, however, development of airplanes progressed dramatically as military leaders realized their value both for surveillance and as weapons.

By the mid 1920s, planes had become more dependable and capable of longer flights. People began to realize their potential as a new form of transportation for both people and cargo.

In 1927, Charles Lindbergh set a cross-country record when he flew from San Diego, California, to New York in 21 hours and 20 minutes. (He stopped overnight at St. Louis, Missouri.) Ten days later, Lindbergh made his most famous flight when he became the first pilot to fly solo across the Atlantic Ocean from New York to Paris, France.

Charles Lindbergh and **The Spirit of St. Louis**

Circle "F" for Fact or "O" for Opinion.

1. F   O   The Wright brothers were really smart.

2. F   O   The first successful airplane flight took place in 1903.

3. F   O   During World War I, better and more dependable airplanes were developed.

4. F   O   Early pilots must have been very brave.

5. F   O   Charles Lindbergh made the first solo trans-Atlantic crossing in an airplane.

6. F   O   Charles Lindbergh was a hero.

7. F   O   Airplanes today are much larger and faster than they were in the 1920s.

8. F   O   Everyone enjoys flying.

Name: ___________________________________ Date: ___________________________

Who's Who?

Many Americans became famous in the 1920s and 1930s. Use reference sources if you need help matching these people with their areas of fame. Some terms may be used more than once, and some people may have more than one term to describe them.

Actress/Actor **Anthropologist** **Artist** **Author** **Baseball player**
Boxer **Composer** **Dancer** **Film maker** **Football player**
Golfer **Magician** **Musician** **Olympic medal winner**
Pilot **Singer** **Tennis player**

1. ___________________________ Marian Anderson

2. ___________________________ Fred Astaire

3. ___________________________ Pearl S. Buck

4. ___________________________ Charlie Chaplin

5. ___________________________ Douglas Corrigan

6. ___________________________ Jack Dempsey

7. ___________________________ Walt Disney

8. ___________________________ Amelia Earhart

9. ___________________________ Duke Ellington

10. ___________________________ George Gershwin

11. ___________________________ Benny Goodman

12. ___________________________ Red Grange

13. ___________________________ Jean Harlow

14. ___________________________ Harry Houdini

15. ___________________________ Bobby Jones

16. ___________________________ Joe Louis

17. ___________________________ Margaret Mead

18. ___________________________ Jelly Roll Morton

19. ___________________________ Jesse Owens

20. ___________________________ Babe Ruth

21. ___________________________ Bessie Smith

22. ___________________________ John Steinbeck

23. ___________________________ Big Bill Tilden

24. ___________________________ Gene Tunney

25. ___________________________ Johnny Weissmuller

Bessie Smith

Johnny Weissmuller

Name: _______________________________________ Date: _______________________________

Fads of the 1920s

One of the things that earned the 1920s a reputation as a wild time in American history was the fascination with fads. Unusual, silly, and sometimes dangerous pasttimes became popular with many people. Most of the time, these were young people who enjoyed doing something different while rebelling against their parents' generation.

Dance marathons went on for hours as couples competed to be the last couple still dancing. The winners often won money or other prizes. Popular dances of the 1920s included the Charleston, Fox-Trot, Lindy-Hop, Shimmy, and the Tango. Some of these were very energetic dances with legs kicking and arms waving. This was one of the reasons young women of the decade, with their bobbed haircuts and short dresses, were nicknamed "flappers."

Other silly crazes included completing crossword puzzles, playing mahjong, swallowing goldfish, playing with yo-yos, jumping on pogo sticks, and playing mini golf. More dangerous stunts included flagpole sitting and barnstorming.

Flagpole sitting involved climbing a flagpole and sitting on a small seat for hours or days at a time. A movie theater owner in Hollywood hired stuntman and former sailor Alvin "Shipwreck" Kelly to sit on a flagpole outside the theater as a publicity stunt in 1924. He sat on the pole for 13 hours and 13 minutes. The stunt was a success at catching people's attention, and soon people of all ages around the country were climbing poles and sitting. Kelly toured the country, holding the record at various times for polesitting. Fifteen-year-old Avon Foreman of Baltimore held the juvenile record with 10 days, 10 hours, and 10 seconds in 1928. Then in September 1929, 14-year-old William Ruppert of Colgate, Maryland, set the record by beating Kelly's 23-day mark. Kelly's longest session was 49 days and one hour in 1930.

William Ruppert after 23 days of flagpole sitting in his backyard in Colgate, Maryland.

Daring barnstorming pilots also thrilled people in the 1920s. After World War I, former military pilots and civilian pilots were able to purchase surplus planes cheaply from the military. The stunt pilots put on shows featuring flying tricks like barrel rolls, loop-the-loops, spins, and dives, all performed at very low altitudes. Aerialists performed tricks such as wing walking and even jumping from plane to plane. The barnstorming name came from the pilots landing in open fields usually near a barn used as the temporary headquarters for the airshow. When several pilots worked together to put on an aerial show, it was called a flying circus. The stunts were very dangerous, and fatal accidents and crashes did happen.

Plan a fun "Fad Day" for your class. Get permission to spend a day or a class period exploring some fun fads. Dress in a particular fashion style, learn one of the latest dance crazes, or compete to become the class record holder. How long can you stand on one leg? How many pennies can you balance on your forehead?

You can research fads of the 1920s and try to come up with activities that incorporate those fads, or you can use the current fads of today. Remember, only perform safe activities!

Name: _________________________________ Date: _________________________________

The Other Side of the Coin

Not everyone in the 1920s had a decade of good times. When people today read about Prohibition, gangsters, speakeasies, bootleg liquor, flappers, slang, dance marathons, and jazz, it's easy to get the impression gangsters hung around every street corner and all Americans partied every night.

Although the decade was marked by fun and extravagance, not everyone lived that way. In fact, the majority of people, especially middle- and lower-class families, probably lived much the way you do now. Children went to school. They did chores around the house. They spent time with friends and family.

For some groups like Black Americans, farmers, and newly-arrived immigrants, the 1920s didn't roar at all. Economic conditions had changed little for Black people in the south since the time of slavery. Prejudice was still strong. Schools and public buildings remained segregated.

Farmers in the 1920s did what farmers have done for thousands of years. They plowed their fields, planted their crops, and prayed for good weather and a good harvest.

Immigrants also met prejudice as they tried to learn a new language, find jobs, and become part of a new country.

Fill in the chart to show similarities and differences between children in the 1920s and children today.

	1920s only	Now only	Then & Now
Attend school			
Watch movies			
Play video games			
Play baseball			
Help around the house			
Play board games like checkers			
Watch TV			
Listen to the radio			
Play with dolls			
Roller skate			
Ride skateboards			
Build snowmen			
Read books			

Name: ____ Date: _________________________________

Evolution on Trial

In 1925, high school biology teacher John T. Scopes was accused of violating the Butler Act. This Tennessee law made it illegal for a teacher in any state-supported public school or college to teach any theory of evolution because it contradicted the Bible's account of man's creation.

Tennessee's Governor Austin Peay said, "The very integrity of the Bible in its statement of man's divine creation is denied by any theory that man descended or has ascended from any lower order of animals."

Opponents to the law believed it was a violation of the Constitution, which insures the separation of church and state.

The trial of John Scopes gained worldwide media attention. Members of the press referred to it as the "Monkey Trial" because many people thought that evolution meant humans had descended from monkeys.

The defense attorney, Clarence Darrow, argued that evolution was a valid scientific theory. He also attempted to convince the jury that the Butler Act was unconstitutional. However, he did not deny that Scopes had broken the law. As a result, Scopes was convicted and fined $100.

Darrow stated that this was "the first case of its kind since we stopped trying people for witchcraft." The verdict was later reversed by the state supreme court, but the Butler Act remained on the books in Tennessee until 1967.

1. Why do you think a trial in Tennessee would gain worldwide attention?

____

____

____

____

2. Clarence Darrow's defense was that the law was wrong. If a law is wrong, do you think that makes it all right to ignore or break it?

____

____

____

____

3. What do you think Darrow meant by the quote above?

____

____

____

____

Name: _______________________________________ Date: _______________________________

Review the Twenties

Match the definition in the right column with the corresponding term in the left column.

_____ 1. Charlie Chaplin

_____ 2. suffrage

_____ 3. ensemble

_____ 4. The Noble Experiment

_____ 5. improvise

_____ 6. Model A

_____ 7. Dixieland

_____ 8. Gertrude Ederle

_____ 9. spiffy

_____ 10. Babe Ruth

A. A group of musicians

B. Baseball player

C. A comedian who starred in movies

D. A type of automobile

E. Dressed up

F. Another term for Prohibition

G. Make up as you go along

H. Right to vote

I. Swam the English Channel

J. A style of jazz

Circle "T" for True or "F" for False.

11. T F The 1920s were nicknamed the Roaring Twenties because people played their radios so loud all of the time.

12. T F During the 1920s, cars had a major influence on Americans.

13. T F Calvin Coolidge's administration was marked by scandal and corruption.

14. T F Charles Lindbergh made the first solo flight across the Atlantic Ocean.

15. T F Women who cut their hair short and wore short skirts and makeup were called flappers.

16. T F Although jazz began in the 1920s, it didn't become popular until the 1960s.

17. T F Warren G. Harding died while president.

18. T F Jazz combined rock and roll, opera, and classical music into a new form.

19. T F Louis Armstrong grew up in a rich home in New York City.

20. T F None of the movies made during the 1920s or 1930s were Westerns.

Name: ___________________________ Date: ___________________________

Herbert Hoover, The Millionaire Miner

Before becoming president, Hoover led a colorful life. Orphaned at the age of eight, he was raised by his uncle in Oregon. While at Stanford University, Hoover founded his own fraternity: the Barbarians.

When Herbert Hoover graduated with a mining engineering degree in 1895, he had $40 in his pocket and no job prospects. He ended up working for $2.50 a day as a pick-and-shovel miner in a California gold mine. His experience, hard work, talents, and ambition did not lack a challenge for long, though.

At age 23, he managed a successful gold mine in Western Australia. From there he went to China as a mining consultant. He spent time with other mining operations in Europe, Russia, Southwest Asia, and Africa.

By 1908, Hoover owned a worldwide business with offices in France, England, and the United States and was a millionaire several times over.

Although he probably could have made another fortune during World War I when the demand for ore and metal increased greatly, Hoover agreed to head the Commission for Relief in Belgium. He worked without pay to organize a successful relief program to feed ten million starving people in Belgium. Then he accepted the position of Food Administrator in the United States and later, Chief of the Supreme Allied Economic Council.

Hoover's success led to his appointment as Secretary of Commerce under Presidents Harding and Coolidge. When President Coolidge chose not to seek reelection in 1928, the Republicans nominated Hoover as their candidate for president.

1. From what you read, what impresses you the most about Herbert Hoover? Explain your answer.

____

____

____

____

2. Why do you think a successful businessman like Hoover would agree to take on the responsibility for feeding ten million people and agree to do it without pay?

____

____

____

____

Name: _______________________________________ Date: _______________________________

The Crash Heard Around the World

People view a stock ticker, which transmitted information on the stock market.

Throughout the 1920s, people spent money much more freely than ever before. More products were available, more people had jobs, and wages were higher. People bought on credit. As stock prices steadily climbed throughout the decade, people often invested everything they had, mortgaged their homes, and even borrowed money to buy stocks. They thought the prosperity of the 1920s would last forever.

In the fall of 1929, investors who had bought stocks on credit began to sell. As more stocks sold, prices fell. Investors panicked, especially those who had bought stocks on margin (bought at a lower price, promising to pay the rest later). Between Black Thursday (October 24, 1929) and Terrible Tuesday (October 29, 1929), so many shares of stock were sold that the market collapsed completely. In one day, stock values dropped $10–$15 billion.

Not all Americans had invested in the stock market, but almost everyone felt an immediate effect of the crash. Most Americans kept their savings in banks that had invested the funds in the stock market. When the stock market crashed, the banks couldn't return the money to investors. In one terrible week, rich, middle-class, and poor people lost everything.

Headline from The Daily Californian on October 29, 1929

Over 1,300 banks went broke in 1930. Another 2,300 failed the following year. The stock market crash brought the good times of the 1920s to a screeching halt. Although no one yet realized the extent of the problem, the stock market crash began the Great Depression, which lasted until the mid 1940s.

Unemployment went from three percent in 1925 to 25 percent in 1932. Many people who still had jobs were required to take pay cuts to keep their jobs.

1. How do you think people felt if they had all their savings in a bank that suddenly went broke?

   ____

   ____

   ____

2. Using a dictionary, state the economic meaning of *depression*.

   ____

   ____

3. On your own paper, create an illustration that summarizes this paragraph:

   As more people lost their jobs, they had less money to spend. Less people spending money meant stores sold fewer products and needed fewer workers. Since fewer products were purchased, factories produced less, and more people lost their jobs.

Name: _________________________________ Date: _______________________

The 1930s and the Beginning of the Great Depression

The 1920s may have begun with a bang, but the 1930s opened with a crash. The effects of the October 1929 Stock Market Crash echoed across the nation as the new decade began. The hard times of the 1930s became known as the Great Depression. During a depression, there is little money and no economic growth.

Investors lost tens of billions of dollars. Over a million people lost their life savings in the stock market crash. Even those who had no money in stocks felt the chain reaction that resulted.

People in the 1930s faced many new challenges as businesses and industries shut down and banks collapsed. When banks closed, many people lost their savings. They had little money, so they bought fewer goods. Therefore, manufacturing slowed because manufacturers could not sell what they had made. Workers then lost their jobs because people were not buying as many products.

Millions of people found themselves unemployed and homeless. Schools closed in rural areas. An estimated 2.2 million children were not attending school in 1933. Between 1930 and 1935, as many as 750,000 farms were lost because of bankruptcy.

President Herbert Hoover underestimated the severity of the problem as he assured people that the crisis was "a passing incident in our national lives." Hoover did not believe the federal government should provide relief or jobs to individuals. He thought private charities, together with city and state governments, were responsible for helping those in need.

During the 1930s, many people relied on soup kitchens for food. They stood in bread lines to buy day-old bread. They looked to the government to solve the massive unemployment problem. Men walked around with their pockets turned inside out to show they were broke. Millions learned to make do with what they had because they couldn't afford new clothing, furniture, appliances, or automobiles.

Soup kitchen for the unemployed in Washington, D.C., 1936

Advances in technology, communications, and transportation continued but at a much slower pace than in the previous decade.

1. Using a dictionary, state what *bankruptcy* means. ____________________________

____

2. Do you agree or disagree with Hoover that charities instead of the government were responsible for those in need? Why?

____

____

____

3. Why do you think advances in technology, communication, and transportation slowed in the 1930s?

____

____

Name: _________________________________ Date: _________________________________

Conduct an Interview

You are a reporter for a newspaper in December 1929. Your boss sent you to write an article about the effects of the stock market crash on one formerly wealthy family who lost everything.

Write 12 questions you could ask someone from that family in an interview for your article.

1. ____

____

2. ____

____

3. ____

____

4. ____

____

5. ____

____

6. ____

____

7. ____

____

8. ____

____

9. ____

____

10. ____

____

11. ____

____

12. ____

____

Name: ____ Date: _______________________________

What's New?

Circle all the products that were introduced in the 1920s and 1930s that people still use today.

1920	Pogo® sticks
1921	Band-Aids® Wrigley's® gum
1922	Eskimo Pie® The *Readers Digest* magazine
1923	Welch's® grape jelly *Time* magazine
1924	Wheaties® cereal spiral-bound notebooks Kleenex® crossword puzzle books permanents for hair
1925	*The New Yorker* magazine
1926	zippers
1927	Hostess® cakes
1928	Rice Krispies®
1930	Nancy Drew mysteries
1931	Scotch® Tape electric razors Scrabble® Alka-Seltzer®

1933	Mickey Mouse® watches comic books
1934	hi-fi records
1935	parking meters paperback books electric typewriters MONOPOLY® game first sold by Parker Brothers
1936	electric guitars *LIFE* magazine
1937	nylon *Look* magazine Wheat Chex®
1938	*Jack and Jill* magazine
1939	air-conditioned cars

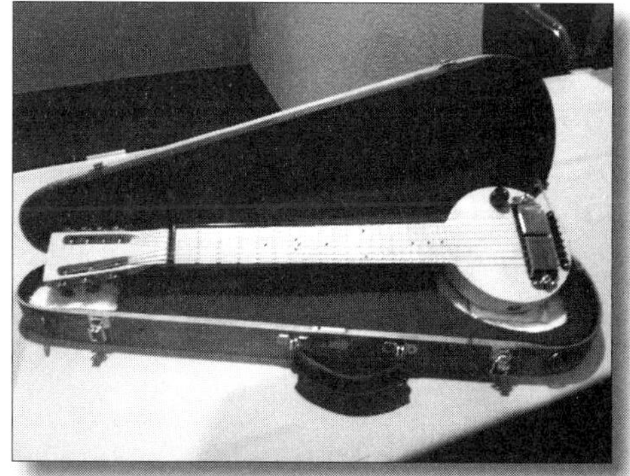

1. Which of these products surprises you the most that it was available so long ago? Why?

____

____

____

Name: _______________________________   Date: _______________________

Herbert Hoover, President

Born: August 10, 1874
Term as President: March 4, 1929, to March 4, 1933
Political Party: Republican

During Herbert Hoover's presidential campaign, the country was flourishing. Most people expected the economic prosperity to continue indefinitely. In a spirit of optimism, Hoover promised "… a chicken in every pot and a car in every garage."

1. What do you think Hoover really meant by that?

____

____

____

____

President Herbert Hoover

Although the economic prosperity of the 1920s continued in most industries until the stock market crash, farmers were already having problems. As they increased efficiency and put more land into farming, prices dropped. Trying to produce more crops made prices drop even lower. In response, Congress passed the Agricultural Marketing Act of 1929, which established the first large-scale aid to farmers during peacetime.

Although Hoover began his term as president on an optimistic note, that ended less than eight months later when the stock market crashed in October 1929, plunging the United States into what became known as the Great Depression.

After the Depression began, farm prices continued to drop. By 1932, government funds ran out, and prices plunged to a new low.

Hoover went from being a very popular president to one of the most disliked men in America. By the 1932 presidential election, the entire country had been affected, leaving Hoover with little chance for reelection.

2. Do you think the Great Depression was Hoover's fault? Why or why not?

____

____

____

3. Would you have voted for Hoover in 1932? Why or why not?

____

____

____

Name: ______________________________　　Date: ______________________________

Meet Young Franklin D. Roosevelt

Born: January 30, 1882, in Hyde Park, New York
Profession: Lawyer
Term as President: March 4, 1933, to April 12, 1945
Political Party: Democratic

Roosevelt during the campaign in 1920

Franklin D. Roosevelt grew up in a wealthy New York family. He spent summers vacationing in Europe and never attended school until he was 14 years old. His family provided private tutors, and his mother supervised his education.

As a young man, Roosevelt enjoyed bird watching and natural history. He enjoyed sports, particularly swimming and hiking, as well as reading adventure stories and stamp collecting.

In 1896, Roosevelt attended Groton School, a private preparatory school in Massachusetts. He went on to Harvard and then to Columbia Law School in 1904. Against his mother's advice, he married Eleanor Roosevelt, a distant cousin.

Roosevelt's early political career included two terms in the New York state senate (1910–1913) and an appointment as assistant secretary of the Navy (1913–1920). He resigned to campaign for the vice presidency in 1920 but lost the election.

As a result of polio in 1921, Roosevelt lost the use of his legs. He was unable to walk without crutches. His mother wanted him to retire from politics, but Roosevelt had other ideas.

With the help of his wife, Roosevelt remained active behind the scenes until he ran for governor of New York in 1928. Most people were unaware of the extent of his disability when he was governor and later president.

1. Use reference sources to find the Democratic candidate who ran for president with Roosevelt in 1920.

   ____

2. Since his family was wealthy, Roosevelt could have retired and spent the rest of his life relying on servants and nurses to care for him. Instead, he chose an active, productive career. What does that tell you about his character?

   ____

   ____

   ____

   ____

Name: _________________________________ Date: _______________________

New President, New Deal

In 1928, the Republican candidate, Herbert Hoover, received the electoral votes from all but seven states. After the Great Depression began, the tide turned. Many people blamed Hoover and the Republicans for the economic problems of the country.

In the 1932 presidential election, only six states remained Republican. Franklin D. Roosevelt, the Democratic candidate, received the electoral votes from 42 states.

1. Draw two pie charts or two of another type of graph to show a comparison between the results of the 1928 and 1932 presidential elections.

To help the country and its people recover, Roosevelt and Congress quickly passed several measures to relieve poverty, reduce unemployment, speed economic recovery, and stabilize the banking industry. Roosevelt's "New Deal" programs didn't provide an immediate cure, but they did ease hard times by addressing basic needs and giving new hope to Americans by setting the groundwork for a gradual recovery.

Although the Great Depression hadn't ended by the time of the 1936 election, voters stayed with Roosevelt and the Democrats. He received the electoral votes from every state except Maine and Vermont.

When George Washington refused to run for a third term as president, he set a precedent that all other presidents followed—until Franklin D. Roosevelt. Not only did Roosevelt run for a third term and win, he was also elected for a fourth term.

2. Why do you think the term "New Deal" was used for Roosevelt's programs?

____

____

____

3. Do you think there should be a limit to how long a person can hold a political office? Why or why not?

____

____

____

Name: _________________________________ Date: _________________________________

President Roosevelt

When Franklin D. Roosevelt took office on March 4, 1933, more than 13,000,000 people were out of work, banks had failed, and the country was in trouble.

Roosevelt immediately called a special session of Congress and pushed for needed legislation to deal with the banking crisis, economic issues, and changes to the liquor law.

President Franklin D. Roosevelt

Roosevelt's domestic New Deal programs introduced reforms that involved the government directly in national and economic affairs. During the first hundred days of his administration, he passed many new programs including the Economy Act, which reduced government salaries and pensions. A new law made low-alcohol beer legal, even though Prohibition was still in effect.

No session of Congress had ever produced so much important legislation. Roosevelt's success was partly due to widespread desperation and partly to his ability as a strong leader.

Roosevelt and his advisors felt it was important that people see him as a strong leader. To minimize his disability, he was seated first at dinners, and his wheelchair was removed before other guests arrived. The press cooperated by not reporting the extent of his physical problems and publishing pictures that showed him standing (which he could do for short periods of time or with the help of a couple of strong men) or seated only in regular chairs. Many people were unaware that he couldn't walk.

Previous presidents had relied heavily on advice from other politicians who belonged to the same political party. Understanding the enormity of the problems facing the nation, Roosevelt turned for advice to a group called the Brain Trust, which were faculty members from Columbia University and Harvard.

1. Do you think the press would conceal a disability for a president or major leader today? Why or why not?

____

____

2. Why do you think Roosevelt didn't want people to know the extent of his disability?

____

____

____

3. Do you think the Brain Trust was a good idea? Why or why not?

____

____

____

Name: _________________________________ Date: _____________________________

The Lame Duck Amendment

The purpose of the Twentieth Amendment, ratified in 1933, was to shorten the time between the election and the date when government officials took office.

Under the original Constitution, a new president and vice president took office on March 4 following the November election. If the incumbent president and vice president had not been reelected or had decided not to run, they remained in office for four months after the election. The Twentieth Amendment moved that date up to January 20.

Newly elected members of Congress had to wait 13 months to take office, as the next regular session of Congress didn't begin until December of the year after the election. In the meantime, those who had not run for office or won reelection retained their positions for over a year. With the change, new members of Congress begin their terms on January 3 following the election.

Section 3 states that if the president-elect dies before taking office, the vice president-elect shall become the president.

The amendment also states that if no president has been selected by January 20, the newly elected vice president shall become acting president until a president is chosen. If neither the president nor vice president has been chosen by January 20, Congress will decide who becomes acting president.

1. Why do you think people wanted to change the dates when the president, vice president, and legislators took office?

____

____

____

2. Why do you think this was called the "Lame Duck" Amendment?

____

____

____

3. Do you think it was fair to allow the newly elected vice president to become president if the president-elect died before taking office? Why or why not?

____

____

____

4. Why is it important to be very specific about who becomes president?

____

____

Name: _______________________________________ Date: _______________________________

Math Facts

1. In 1933, the minimum wage was set at 40 cents an hour. How much would _______________ a person earn each week working 10 hours a day, six days a week?

2. What would that person's annual income be? _______________

3. The first parking meter was installed in Oklahoma City, Oklahoma, in _______________ 1935. How many years ago was that?

4. There were 750 miles of paved roads in the United States in 1909. By _______________ 1930, that number had gone up to 100,000 miles. On an average, how many miles of road would have had to be built per year during that 21-year time period? Round your answer to the nearest mile.

5. The world-famous Mickey Mouse® watch first became available in 1933. _______________ It sold for $2.75. At 40 cents an hour, how long would a person have to work to pay for a Mickey Mouse® watch? Round your answer to the nearest hour.

6. In 1937, wages for workers at U.S. Steel were raised to $5 a day. How _______________ much did they earn per hour if they worked ten-hour days?

7. The U.S. Treasury Department announced in October 1925 that they had _______________ fined 29,620 people for Prohibition (alcohol) violations. The fines totaled $5,000,000. What was the average amount of fine per person? Round your answer to the nearest dollar.

8. Herbert Hoover's first job after college was as a pick-and-shovel miner _______________ for $2.50 a day. How much did he earn for a six-day workweek?

9. Working with a friend, Charles Darrow could make six copies of his version _______________ of the MONOPOLY® game in a day. He sold the games for $4 each. How much money would they have made if they sold all the games they made in 15 days?

10. In 1924, a Ford Model T sold for $290. The Model A introduced in 1927 _______________ sold for $395. What was the percent of increase in the cost? Round your answer to the nearest percent.

11. In 1920, less than 15 percent of the people in the United States had a _______________ telephone. The population of the United States in 1920 was 105,710,620. What is 15 percent of that number?

12. By 1930, the population of the United States had risen to 122,775,046. _______________ How many more people were there than in 1920?

Name: _______________________________ Date: _______________________________

The Repeal of Prohibition

The Eighteenth Amendment prohibiting alcohol was ratified by voters in three-quarters of the states, yet no law was ever so violently opposed and ignored at all levels of American society. As a result, many people felt Prohibition promoted disrespect for the law.

1. Do you agree or disagree? Why?

____

____

____

Almost as soon as Prohibition was passed, people began working to repeal it. They felt that the law was an invasion of the private lives of citizens.

2. Do you agree or disagree? Why?

____

____

____

Another argument for repeal was that Prohibition generated organized crime and that the profits that could be made from illegal alcohol promoted corruption at almost every level of government.

3. Do you agree or disagree? Why?

____

____

____

In 1933, Section 1 of the Twenty-First Amendment to the Constitution ended Prohibition. According to Section 2, if any state, territory, or possession of the United States wanted to make alcohol illegal, they had the right to do so. It would then be illegal to import or manufacture alcohol in those areas.

4. Write three reasons of your own why alcohol should or should not be illegal.

____

____

____

____

Name: _________________________________ Date: _______________________

Isolationism

During much of its history, the United States has maintained an **isolationist** policy, believing the country's best interest would be served by avoiding alliances with other nations. This policy of isolationism kept the United States out of World War I until 1917. When the United States finally declared war, leaders felt our country was obligated to "make the world safe for democracy."

After World War I, President Woodrow Wilson presented a plan for a general association of nations that became the League of Nations in 1920. Although Wilson was a member of the committee that drafted the charter, the U.S. Senate never ratified it.

Article X of the charter stated that if any nation threatened a member country, all members of the league would be obligated to help, even if it meant war. American diplomats encouraged the league's activities and unofficially attended meetings, but the United States never became a member of the League of Nations.

World War I was called "the war to end all wars." However, it soon became clear that all countries would not be democracies and nations would continue to fight wars. Faced with the problems of the Great Depression, the tendency towards isolationism increased. Many people decided to ignore the problems in other countries, choosing rather to focus on and solve problems at home.

During the 1930s, new dictators rose in Germany, Japan, Italy, and Russia, causing a flood of immigration to the United States. Instead of welcoming new arrivals, Congress cut the number of allowed immigrants in an effort to control and restrict foreign influences. In the early 1930s, Congress also voted to restrict foreign trade to protect the U.S. economy and to remain neutral in foreign disputes.

1. What do you think the phrase "make the world safe for democracy" means?

   ____

   ____

   ____

2. If you had been a member of the Senate, would you have voted to join the League of Nations? Why or why not?

   ____

   ____

   ____

3. Do you agree or disagree with the policy of isolationism? Why?

   ____

   ____

   ____

Name: _________________________________ Date: _______________________

What Happened When?

Use the timeline on page 3 to complete this activity.

1. When and where were the first Winter Olympics in the U.S. held?

   ____

2. What were two magazines first published in the 1930s?

   ____

3. What was the title of Disney's first full-length animated movie?

   ____

4. Who was the president in 1937? ___________________________________

5. When did the "The Star-Spangled Banner" become the official national anthem?

   ____

6. How many homes in the United States had radios in 1934?

   ____

7. Which opened first, the Golden Gate Bridge or
   the Empire State Building?

   ____

8. How much did it cost to mail a letter in 1932?

   ____

9. Who was the first woman to become a member
   of the president's Cabinet?

   ____

10. How many people were unemployed in 1932?

    ____

11. What was minimum wage in 1933? _________________________________

12. Which amendment repealed the Prohibition amendment? _______________

13. When was the Social Security Act signed? _______________________

14. Which were available first: electric guitars, electric typewriters, or electric calculators?

    ____

15. What was the name of the first published comic book? _______________

    ____

Name: _______________________________________ Date: _______________________________

Fun Facts About the Thirties

- In 1930, Charles Creighton and Jim Hagis made the record books when they drove from New York to Los Angeles and back. That wasn't the first time such a trip had been undertaken. But it was the first time anyone did it driving backwards all the way! They never drove faster than 14 miles an hour, and the trip took a total of 42 days.

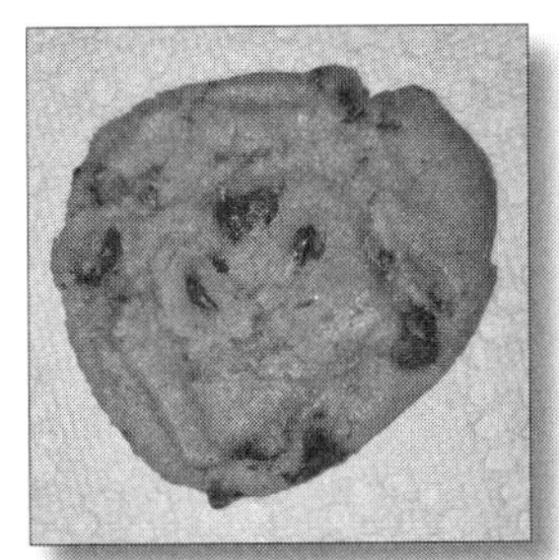

- Ruth Wakefield, owner of the Toll House Inn in Whitman, Massachusetts, invented chocolate chip cookies by accident in 1930. Because she had run out of baking cocoa to make chocolate cookies for her guests, she substituted small pieces of a Nestle's Chocolate Bar. Instead of chocolate cookies, she invented a delicious surprise. In return for allowing them to print her recipe for Toll House Cookies on the candy wrapper, the Nestle Company offered her a lifetime supply of free chocolate.

- Reading became a popular form of entertainment during the 1930s. Penguin Books, launched in England in 1935, pioneered the "paperback revolution" by publishing inexpensive classics and new novels.

- "Elm Farm Ollie" became the first cow to fly in an airplane in 1930. While in flight over St. Louis, the cow was milked. The milk was sealed in little paper containers and then parachuted over the city.

- The first U.S. federal tax on gasoline was enacted in 1932. The rate back then was a penny per gallon!

- Pinball machines were illegal in Atlanta, Georgia, in 1939.

- A U.S. Congressman introduced a resolution in 1932 requiring all Civil Service employees to "sing, write or recite the words to 'The Star-Spangled Banner'" by memory.

- The June 7, 1938, cover of *LIFE* magazine showed the latest in campus fashions of the day, which included saddle shoes.

- Walt Disney's famous duck made his first appearance on film in 1934 as a minor character in "The Wise Little Hen." Donald Duck went on to quack his way to stardom.

- In 1939, the King and Queen of England visited President and Mrs. Franklin D. Roosevelt. In honor of the grand event, the White House staff prepared gourmet foods of the United States. It was the first time the King and Queen tasted hot dogs.

Use the Internet or other reference sources to find two other fun facts about the 1930s. Write them on your own paper.

Name: _______________________________________ Date: _______________________________

New Deal Programs

One popular New Deal program was the **Civilian Conservation Corps (CCC)**. Established by Congress in 1933, the CCC provided needy young men with jobs in forests and national parks.

Civilian Conservation Corps workers planting trees, c. 1933

The program had two main purposes: employment and training for young men, and conservation of natural resources including timber, soil, and water. Unemployed, unmarried men between the ages of 17 and 23 were eligible to join the CCC. They were paid $30 a month and lived in work camps. About three million men were employed by the CCC.

Workers carved out roads and hiking trails, cleaned up beaches, and cleared camping sites to develop national parks. They laid down telephone lines and constructed fire observation towers. Reforestation projects included planting about two million trees from Texas to North Dakota.

The **Works Progress Administration (WPA)** began in 1935 when the president and Congress decided to shift federal relief funds to providing useful employment. By 1943, the program had provided jobs for nine million workers in road maintenance and construction of buildings and facilities. The **National Youth Administration (NYA)** program also provided four million part-time jobs.

Projects included the construction of schools, dormitories, hospitals, airports, docks, and ports plus slum clearance, flood control, and rural electrification. The WPA also provided jobs for artists (painting murals on public buildings), writers (conducting research projects), and actors and actresses (touring and performing in rural areas) through the Federal Writers, Theater, and Arts Program.

1. Why do you think the CCC was a very popular program? _________________________________

   ____

   ____

2. How did the work done by members of the CCC help all Americans?

   ____

   ____

3. Do you think it is the government's obligation to provide work for people who are unemployed? Why or why not?

   ____

   ____

4. What do you think is better: providing jobs or providing direct relief payments? Why?

   ____

   ____

Name: ___________________________________ Date: _______________________

An Alphabet Soup of New Deal Programs

Besides the CCC, the WPA, and the NYA, Roosevelt's New Deal included a whole alphabet soup of other programs. Even Roosevelt himself was often referred to as FDR.

Use reference sources to find the answers.

One of Roosevelt's earliest concerns was to stabilize banks and give depositors a sense of security. The FDIC insured the savings of depositors up to $5,000 at all Federal Reserve banks.

1. What does FDIC stand for? ____

The TVA was authorized to manage local resources and construct a series of hydroelectric dams to provide cheap power.

2. What does TVA stand for? ____

Created in 1933, FERA granted three billion dollars to states to fund work projects for unemployed adults.

3. What does FERA stand for?

____

____

Typists at a FERA camp in Pennsylvania, 1934

The AAA provided crop reduction subsidies to stabilize prices and loans for overdue farm mortgages.

4. What does AAA stand for? ____

Another federal program, the HOLC, helped people in danger of losing their homes due to foreclosure by allowing them to refinance with low-interest loans.

5. What does HOLC stand for? ____

The NRA was designed to assist industry and labor by establishing voluntary codes and standards for wages, working hours, child labor, etc. As a whole, this program had many faults, but it did bring about shorter workdays and five-day workweeks.

6. What does NRA stand for? (Note: this was not the National Rifle Association.)

____

Name: _______________________________________ Date: _______________________________

Desperate Times, Desperate People, Desperate Actions

When the International Apple Shippers Association came up with an oversupply of fruit in 1930, they also came up with a unique solution. They sold apples on credit to people who were unemployed. The unemployed stood on street corners selling apples for five cents each.

This trend led to others besides apple sellers peddling everything from watches to patent medicines. Cities eventually had to pass laws banning street vendors as a public nuisance.

People who were desperate sometimes turned to pawnshops. In exchange for a ring, watch, or other treasured item, pawnshops might loan a person a few dollars to buy groceries, pay the rent, or keep their car from being repossessed.

In March 1933, about 1,000 people a day all across the country lost their homes due to foreclosures. When people couldn't pay their rent or mortgages, they were evicted from their homes.

Desperate for places to live, people moved into abandoned factories and warehouses. Shanty towns called **Hoovervilles** sprang up in empty lots, under bridges, in city dumps, and along major highways.

People scrounged through city dumps, construction sites, and trash bins for materials to build shelters. Abandoned cars and stacks of wooden fruit boxes became homes for desperate families.

Shanties in a Hooverville on the Seattle waterfront, 1933

They lacked electricity and running water. Crime, disease, and hunger filled these shanty towns.

Those who managed to keep or find jobs often had to take a cut in pay and/or a cut in hours. People took in boarders to help pay the bills and share expenses. Women and children worked when they could. People begged when they had no other choice.

Black Americans and immigrants were affected as much or more by the lack of jobs. Often the last hired and the first fired, they earned less, worked harder, and had less job security even in good times. Black people who had been tenant farmers in the South migrated to the North hoping to find work.

1. How did the Apple Shippers Association's solution help the Association, consumers, and the unemployed?

   ____

   ____

   ____

2. Why do you think the shanty towns were nicknamed Hoovervilles or Hoover Cities?

   ____

   ____

   ____

Name: _______________________________ Date: _____________________________

Major Projects of the Depression Era

The Tennesse Valley Authority (TVA) was established in 1933. Eventually, the TVA built 30 dams on the Tennessee River and its tributaries. Nine of the high dams created huge man-made lakes, such as Kentucky Lake. The dams helped control flooding and provided electrical power to poor regions. Parks were created, trees and grass were planted over eroded areas, and soil fertility was restored. This brought a new way of life to the people of the Tennessee River valley, improving travel on the Tennessee River and helping agriculture and industry in the region. Thousands of jobs were created by the TVA projects. Workers with the Civilian Conservation Corps (CCC) also worked on state parks in the region and environmental parts of the project.

Originally authorized in 1928, the Hoover Dam received Public Works Administration (PWA) funding. The federal government ended up providing about 27% of the $140 million cost. Although it was known as Boulder Dam for many years after an earlier proposed building site, the dam was built across Black Canyon in Nevada about 37 miles from Las Vegas. The dam was built to control the flooding of the Colorado River and to distribute water for agriculture and cities in seven southwestern states: Colorado, Wyoming, Utah, New Mexico, Arizona, Nevada, and California. The 726.4-foot tall dam was constructed with 6.6 million tons of concrete by approximately 21,000 workers. It has 17 turbines that generate enough electricity to power 1.3 million homes. The damming of the Colorado River formed Lake Mead, the largest reservoir lake in the United States. The dam and lake also created a tourist and recreation destination for the area.

Hoover Dam

The Lincoln Tunnel, which connects New Jersey with the New York City borough of Manhattan, was drilled under the Hudson River. The first tube of the tunnel, providing two-way traffic, was completed in 1937. It was funded by the PWA. The 1.5-mile long tunnel was created by workers called sandhogs drilling through the silt and rock under the Hudson River. As material was dug and blasted out from behind a metal shield at the forward edge of the tube, huge metal rings weighing 21 tons each were installed along the wall of the tunnel as the lining. Then cement was poured behind the lining to seal out any water from the river. Workers had to pass through multiple compression and decompression chambers as they made their way down to depths of about 91 feet. Each worker could only handle the pressure for a short time so they had to be changed out frequently. Crews worked from the New Jersey side and the New York side to meet in the middle. A second tube was completed in 1945 and a third in 1957.

The Lincoln Tunnel while under construction in 1936

Other major projects completed during the Great Depression include the Triborough Bridge (now named the Robert F. Kennedy Bridge) in New York City, the Grand Coulee Dam on the Columbia River in the state of Washington, the Golden Gate Bridge in San Francisco, and the Overseas Highway in the Florida Keys.

Name: _______________________________________ Date: _______________________________

Major Projects of the Depression Era (cont.)

Funding and workers from the PWA, WPA, and CCC were also used for many smaller projects such as reforestation and irrigation projects and building post offices, libraries, parks, and other public facilities across the country. Architects, artists, and other creative people were also hired to design and decorate public spaces.

1. Match the location in the second column with the corresponding project in the first column.

   ____ a. Lincoln Tunnel   1. Colorado River

   ____ b. Golden Gate Bridge   2. Florida Keys

   ____ c. Hoover Dam   3. Tennessee River

   ____ d. Grand Coulee Dam   4. Hudson River

   ____ e. Tennessee Valley Authority 5. San Francisco, California

   ____ f. Overseas Highway   6. New York City, New York

   ____ g. Robert F. Kennedy Bridge   7. Columbia River

2. Do some research and find a building, park, or other structure in your area that was built during the Great Depression using funding and workers from one of the New Deal agencies or programs.

   a. Describe the project briefly. ____

   ____

   ____

   ____

   ____

   ____

   b. When was it completed? ____

   c. What agency, agencies, or programs were involved? _________________________

   ____

   ____

   ____

Name: _______________________________________ Date: _______________________________

Let's Listen to the Radio

After the stock market crash of 1929, radio broadcasting was one of the few businesses that prospered during hard times. With millions out of work and money for recreation scarce, radio provided cheap entertainment. Radio also brought people from different classes and different parts of the country together in a new way. Farmers in Iowa could listen to the same music as party-goers in New York. A poor woman in Mississippi could enjoy the same radio adventures as a rich man in California.

Besides live music and records, people listened to political speeches, sports programs, and weather forecasts. Franklin D. Roosevelt kept Americans informed with a series of "fireside chats" to encourage people that the situation in the country was gradually improving.

Orson Welles as The Shadow

Radio also brought situation comedies and dramas into the homes of millions of Americans. Soap operas dominated the daytime airwaves. The most popular program of the 1930s was "Amos 'n' Andy," which attracted as many as 30 million listeners each week.

Other popular serials were "Fibber McGee and Molly," "Little Orphan Annie," "The Green Hornet," "The Shadow," "Jack Armstrong, All-American Boy," "Dick Tracy," and "The Lone Ranger." Many radio stars like Jack Benny went on to make names for themselves in movies and TV. In radio, a person's voice and personality were important, but how they looked didn't matter. The audience could imagine the character any way they wished, based on what they heard.

Besides providing entertainment and information, radio also broadcast advertisements. Even if people couldn't afford new products, they could listen to descriptions and dream of the day when their lives might be better.

One illustration of the impact radio had on Americans was the October 30, 1938, broadcast of the science fiction play "War of the Worlds" about the invasion of Martians. A million listeners panicked as they mistook the play for a newscast.

1. What types of programs did people listen to in the 1930s that people can still hear today?

____

____

2. People in the 1930s relied on the radio for information and entertainment. What sources do people rely on today?

____

3. How did movies and television affect the importance of the appearance of the characters?

____

____

Name: _______________________________________ Date: _______________________________

Meet Eleanor Roosevelt

Use reference sources to fill in the blanks.

Eleanor Roosevelt became the most active first lady up to that time.

1. Although she grew up in a wealthy family, Eleanor Roosevelt's childhood must have been far from happy. When she was eight years old, her _________________ died, and she went to live with her _________________ _________________, a very stern woman.

2. Eleanor was deeply attached to her father, an alcoholic who was often away for treatments and was seldom allowed to visit her. He died when she was _________ years old.

3. Eleanor was sent to a boarding school in _________________ when she was 15.

4. Long before her husband, _________________, was elected president, Eleanor had been an active woman, interested in politics and social conditions. She did charity work in Albany, New York, and worked for the Red Cross during World War I.

5. Unlike most previous first ladies, Eleanor Roosevelt did not believe in staying quietly in the background. She traveled extensively visiting hospitals and schools, held weekly press conferences, and wrote articles and a newspaper column titled, "_________________."

6. Eleanor seemed to enjoy adventure. At the Winter Olympics at Lake Placid, New York, she took a ride down the bobsled run. She rode over _________________ Dam in a bucket. On her way to the Democratic National Convention in 1940, the pilot let her fly the plane.

7. Never one to back away from controversial issues, Eleanor took a stand when members of the Daughters of the American Revolution prevented Marian Anderson, an African American singer, from performing at Constitution Hall in Washington, D.C., in 1939. Angrily, Eleanor resigned from the group and organized an alternate site for the concert at the _________________ _________________.

8. Eleanor remained active after her husband's death and became the U.S. delegate to the _________________ _________________ from 1945 to 1953.

9. What was Eleanor Roosevelt's maiden name? _________________________________

10. Who was her famous uncle? _________________________________

Name: ____ Date: ________________________________

From Rags to Riches

When Charles Darrow lost his job as a salesman of heating and engineering equipment, he tried to support his family by taking any kind of work he could get, but it wasn't enough. He spent his free time inventing toys and games. He had several interesting ideas, but no one was willing to buy them.

Remembering the "good old days" when he and his wife had visited a seaside resort in Atlantic City, New Jersey, Darrow sketched out the street names. He added railroads to carry vacationers to the resort and utilities to service the area. He divided the streets into parcels worth varying amounts. Darrow made little houses and hotels with scraps of wooden molding discarded by a lumber yard. He painted the board and typed title cards for the properties. He used colored buttons for game pieces, dice, and lots of play money. He called the game MONOPOLY®.

Not only did Darrow and his wife enjoy MONOPOLY®, but when friends played, they also liked the game so much they wanted their own sets. Darrow made copies for them. Soon the demand increased, and he began selling the games for $4 each. As more people played MONOPOLY® with their friends, Darrow got more orders and began making two games a day. Encouraged, Darrow made up a few sets and offered them to a department store in Philadelphia. They sold.

Darrow and a friend increased production to six sets a day, but orders piled up faster than they could fill them. Darrow knew he would either have to borrow money to go into production on a larger scale or sell the game to another company.

He wrote to the Parker Brothers game company. They turned him down because they felt MONOPOLY® was too complicated and took too long to play. It would never be accepted by the public, they said.

Darrow enlisted the help of a printer to produce 5,000 sets. Department stores ordered so many sets Darrow found himself working 14 hours a day. A major New York toy and game store (F.A.O. Schwartz) bought 200 sets.

When a friend called Sally Barton (daughter of George Parker) to rave about the marvelous game he had bought in New York, she told her husband, who was currently president of the company. They tried the game, and they found themselves playing it until 1:00 A.M.

Barton wrote to Darrow and met with him three days later. Parker Brothers offered to buy the game and pay royalties on all sets sold on condition that they could make some revisions in the rules. Darrow agreed. The royalties from sales of MONOPOLY® allowed Darrow to retire as a millionaire at the age of 46.

It was later discovered that Darrow developed MONOPOLY® after playing a version of The Landlord's Game®. This game had been developed by Elizabeth J. Magie and patented in 1904. The game was popular with students on college campuses since it was originally created to demonstrate the economic effects of monopolies in real estate. Although Parker Brothers produced some of Magie's other games, she was not given credit for inventing the game that inspired MONOPOLY®. Her role was rediscovered during research for a court case against Parker Brothers by another game inventor in the 1970s.

Work with a small group to invent your own board game. Draw it on poster board. It could be similar to MONOPOLY® using places in your city or based on another theme, like a sport, movie, book, or cartoon character. Gather any game pieces needed, write up the rules, and play the game.

Name: _________________________________ Date: _________________________________

The Thirties: Cause and Effect

A **cause** is an event that produces a result. An **effect** is the result produced. For each cause, write a possible effect.

Cause   **Effect**

1. Banks across the country closed after the stock market crashed.

    ____

    ____

    ____

2. Parts of the country experienced a drought for several years.

    ____

    ____

    ____

3. Millions of people were unemployed during the 1930s.

    ____

    ____

    ____

4. Eleanor Roosevelt was a very active first lady.

    ____

    ____

    ____

5. Congress set up work programs like the CCC and WPA.

    ____

    ____

    ____

6. The Lame Duck Amendment changed the date new members of Congress took office.

    ____

    ____

    ____

Name: ________________________________ Date: ______________________________

Thirties Scavenger Hunt

Use the Internet and other reference sources to find the answers below.

Herbert Hoover's vice president, Charles Curtis, was a Native American.

1. To what tribe did he belong? ____

In 1930, this baseball great signed a two-year contract with the New York Yankees for the huge sum of $80,000.

2. Who was he? ____

An actor who later became a national political figure made his movie debut in 1937 when he was 26 years old in the Warner Brothers movie *Love Is on the Air.*

3. What was his name? ____

In May 1932, Public Enemy Number One, Al Capone, was sent to the Atlanta Penitentiary.

4. Of what crime was he convicted? ____

The first episode of "The Lone Ranger" was heard on radio in 1933, and the show ran until 1954. Several different radio actors played the part of the Lone Ranger, including Clayton Moore from 1949 to 1952. The part of his faithful companion, Tonto, was played for almost the entire time by John Todd, a bald Irishman. On radio and later on television and in films, every episode of "The Lone Ranger" began with the same music.

"The Lone Ranger" TV show

5. What was the name of the song?

____

6. Who played Tonto after it became a TV show?

____

Before the "Singing Cowboy" became famous in movies in the 1930s, he worked as a telegraph operator. He made more than 90 Westerns during his career and had a TV show that ran for six seasons.

7. Who was the "Singing Cowboy"? ____

Fred Waring invented the Waring Blender. However, he was more famous for his other occupation.

8. What was Fred Waring's occupation? ____

Band leader and clarinetist Artie Shaw became famous in the 1930s.

9. What was Artie Shaw's real name? ____

Name: _________________________________ Date: _________________________

The Social Security Act of 1935

Another important law passed while Franklin Roosevelt was president was the Social Security Act of 1935. This act set up six specific programs and established methods of taxes to fund them.

Old-Age Benefits (later called Social Security) was funded by federal taxes deducted from workers. When workers retired at age 65, they became eligible to receive a monthly check. Benefits were extended to widows and dependent children of retired workers.

States taxed employers to fund the **Unemployment Compensation** program to provide income when people were out of work.

The other four programs were forms of welfare funded by grants from the federal government and administered by the states. They included **Old-Age Assistance**, **Aid to Dependent Children**, **Maternal and Child Welfare**, and **Aid to the Blind**.

Old-Age Assistance and Aid to the Blind programs were designed to supplement Old-Age Benefits or to provide benefits for those not eligible for Old-Age Benefits. Maternal and Child Welfare provided health care to poor mothers and their children and was designed to protect and care for homeless, neglected, or disabled children. Aid to Dependent Children helped support children living with only one parent or with relatives other than parents.

The first Social Security cards were issued in 1937 when the government began collecting Social Security taxes. Each person received a unique number used to keep track of earnings and taxes paid. Money was placed into a trust fund to be used to pay benefits, cover the costs of administering the program, and earn interest to build up the fund. To build up the fund, people who retired before 1940 received only one lump sum payment rather than monthly benefits.

1. Which program was funded by taxes on employers?

   ____

2. Which program was not administered by the states?

   ____

3. Which of these six programs do you think was the best? Why?

   ____

   ____

   ____

   ____

4. Do you think it's right for people working today to pay extra taxes to support workers who have retired? Why or why not?

   ____

   ____

   ____

   ____

The Dust Bowl

Life had always been difficult for home-steaders on the Great Plains. Farms were small and water scarce with no reservoirs or irrigation systems. Even in good years, many were lucky to break even.

Dust built up on a farm in 1936

Before farmers moved to the area in the late 1800s, the land was covered with hardy grasses that held the fine-grained soil in place even during times of drought, wind, or torrential rains.

When large numbers of homesteaders settled in the region, they plowed up the grasses and planted crops. The cattle they raised ate whatever grass was left. This exposed the soil to the winds that constantly swept across the flat plains. When a series of droughts hit the area in the early 1930s, combined with the farming practices of the past 50 years, there was nothing to hold the soil in place.

A large area in the southern part of the Great Plains region of the United States came to be known as the **Dust Bowl** during the 1930s. Much of this area suffered extensively from soil erosion.

The Depression had already caused the price of wheat and corn to fall to all-time lows. When crops failed, farmers couldn't make mortgage payments on their farms. By 1932, a thousand families a week were losing their farms in Texas, Oklahoma, and Arkansas. Thousands of families migrated west in search of a better life.

In 1935, both the federal and state governments began developing programs to conserve the soil and reclaim the area. This included seeding large areas with grass; the rotation of wheat, then sorghum, and then lying fallow; contour plowing; terracing; and strip planting. In some areas, "shelter belts" of trees were planted to break the force of the wind.

Use a dictionary to define these words.

1. reservoir: ____

2. irrigation: ____

3. erosion: ____

4. drought: ____

5. Learn more about one of the methods for conserving the soil or reclaiming the land listed in the previous paragraph. On your own paper, explain how it works and how it can help prevent soil loss.

Name: ________________________ Date: ________________________

Conditions Get Worse

The problems in the Dust Bowl area increased in 1936 when the winds began blowing almost continuously. People fled to shelter as huge clouds of dust advanced on them. Dust was carried great distances by the wind, in some cases darkening the sky all the way to the Atlantic Ocean.

During the next four years, as much as three to four inches of topsoil blew away, leaving only hard, red clay, which made farming impossible. Sand settled around homes, fences, and barns. People slept with wet cloths over their faces to filter out the dust. They woke to find themselves, their pillows, and blankets caked with dirt. Animals were buried alive or choked to death on the dust.

People died if they remained outside too long during a dust storm. Many also died from what came to be called "dust pneumonia"—severe damage to the lungs caused by breathing dust.

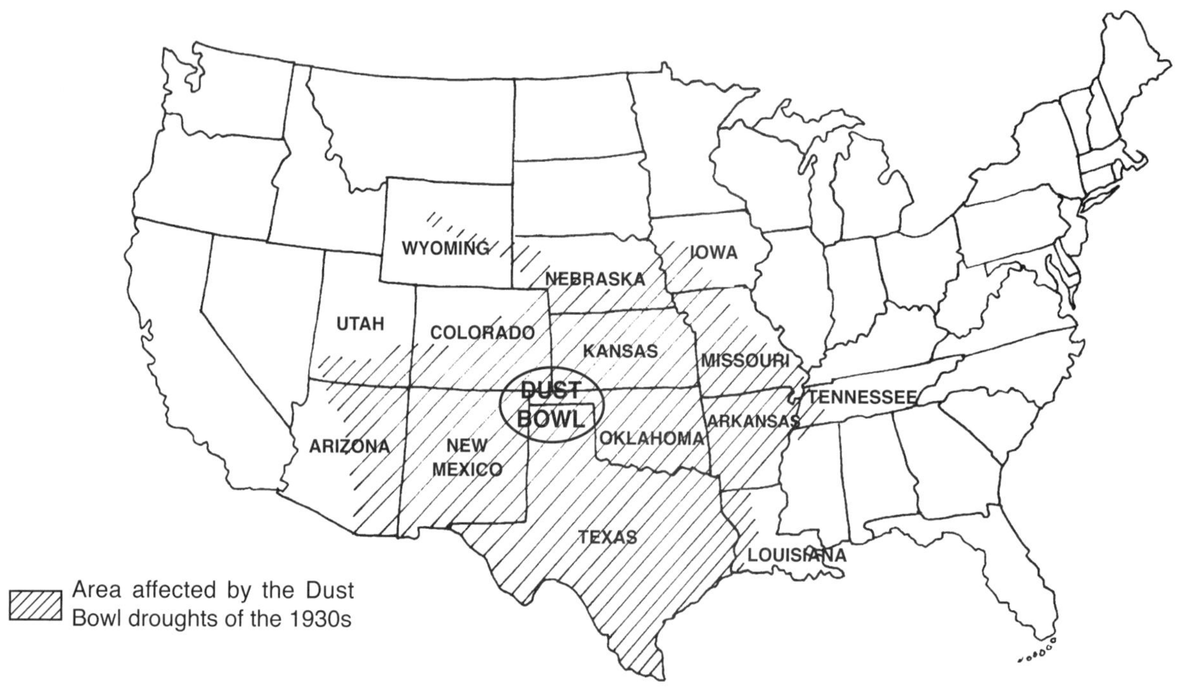

1. Centered in northern Texas, the panhandle of Oklahoma, and southwestern Kansas, the Dust Bowl also included all or part of which other states?

____

____

____

2. Which three states in the area affected by the Dust Bowl were farthest north?

____

3. Which four states were completely in the area affected by the Dust Bowl?

____

Name: _______________________________________ Date: _______________________________

A Cottage for Sale

Music in the 1930s reflected both pessimism due to economic conditions and optimism for a better time to come. People listened to upbeat songs like "Bye, Bye Blues," "Sunny Side Up," and "Get Happy" as well as songs with more serious themes, like "Brother, Can You Spare a Dime?"

Words from **"A Cottage for Sale"** recorded by Guy Lombardo in 1930 can be found in the puzzle. (At that time a cottage meant a small house, not a vacation place.) Look up, down, backward, forward, and diagonally to find and circle the words printed in bold.

Our **little dream castle** with **every** dream **gone**,
Is **lonely and silent**, the **shades** are all **drawn**,
And my **heart** is **heavy** as I **gaze upon**
A **cottage** for **sale**.

The **lawn** we were **proud** of is **waving** in **hay**,
Our **beautiful garden** has **withered away**.
Where **you planted roses**, the **weeds seem** to **say**,
A cottage for sale.

From every **single window**, I **see** your **face**,
But when I reach a window, there's **empty space**.
The key's in the **mail** box the same as **before**,
But no one is **waiting any more**.
The **end** of the **story** is **told** on the **door**,
A cottage for sale.

```
B Y N F E C A P S L I A M A D
E E A W A N O G N I V A W E R
F S A S A C O T T Z E A T E A
O A T U S L E G T R Y N Z Y W
R L I T T L E D D A A A L V N
E E L G N I S K E L G E Y A H
S E S O R T F D P R N E H E W
H T V O N O P U J O E S N H O
A Z O E R O M O L Y E H D D D
D D L R R G A R D E N L T N N
E I U O Y Y T P M E O A A I I
S D E E W V W A I T I N G U W
```

Name: _______________________________________ Date: _______________________________

Review of the Thirties

Match the definition in the right column with the corresponding term in the left column.

_______	1. reservoir	A. Provided jobs for young, unemployed single men
_______	2. erosion	B. A system used to carry water to where it is needed for crops
_______	3. bankruptcy	C. A long period of time with little or no rain
_______	4. Social Security Act	D. A place to hold surplus water for later use
_______	5. Lame Duck Amendment	E. Broke; having no money; unable to pay debts
_______	6. irrigation	F. Provided Old-Age Benefits
_______	7. drought	G. Wearing away of soil due to wind or rain
_______	8. Civilian Conservation Corps	H. Changed date of presidential inauguration

Circle "T" for True or "F" for False.

9. T F Isolationism is a disease that causes people to sleep a lot.

10. T F Franklin D. Roosevelt was elected president four times.

11. T F The thirties were called the Great Depression Era because most people were sad during those years.

12. T F The Dust Bowl was an annual football game played between the top two college teams in Texas.

13. T F Franklin D. Roosevelt was a Democrat.

14. T F During the Depression, people were often hungry. To show they had no food, they put empty bowls on the table and called them Dust Bowls.

15. T F Many flourishing cities were named Hooverville or Hoovertown in honor of Herbert Hoover.

16. T F Many of Roosevelt's New Deal programs were aimed at helping those who were unemployed.

17. T F MONOPOLY® was invented by a rich businessman.

18. T F Radio brought music, news, weather, sports, dramas, comedies, and soap operas into millions of homes during the Depression.

Name: _________________________________   Date: _________________________________

Then and Now

Read the statements about conditions during the Great Depression. Add a statement about conditions today.

1. **Then:** Millions of people were unemployed.

    Now: ____

    ____

    ____

2. **Then:** Millions of people were homeless.

    Now: ____

    ____

    ____

3. **Then:** Listening to the radio and going to the movies were favorite pastimes.

    Now: ____

    ____

    ____

4. **Then:** MONOPOLY® and Scrabble® were popular board games. Children enjoyed playing with dolls, toy cars, blocks, and toy planes.

    Now: ____

    ____

    ____

5. **Then:** People enjoyed listening to jazz and dancing to Big Band music.

    Now: ____

    ____

    ____

6. **Then:** Franklin D. Roosevelt was president.

    Now: ____

    ____

    ____

Name: _________________________________ Date: _________________________________

What Else Happened Then?

Use reference sources to find one historical event for each year that occurred in the United States during the 1930s that was unrelated to the Great Depression or the Dust Bowl.

1930: ____

____

1931: ____

____

1932: ____

____

1933: ____

____

1934: ____

____

1935: ____

____

1936: ____

____

1937: ____

____

1938: ____

____

1939: ____

____

____

Name: ___________________________________   Date: ___________________________

Read All About It!

Option 1: Read a fiction or nonfiction book about the Roaring Twenties or Great Depression.
Option 2: Read a biography of someone who played a role in history at that time.
(See the Suggested Reading books on page 62 for some ideas.)

Title and author of the book: ____

____

Was the book fiction or nonfiction? ____

What years were covered in the book? ____

Briefly describe the main character. ____

____

____

Where did the main character live? ____

Summarize two major events described in the book. ___________________________

____

____

____

____

What was the major problem the main character had to face? __________________

____

____

How was that problem resolved? If it wasn't resolved, why not? ______________

____

____

____

Did you like the book? Why or why not? ______________________________________

____

____

Name: _________________________________ Date: _________________________________

History Projects

Complete one of these projects. Work alone, with a partner, or with a small group if appropriate.

- Create a detailed timeline of the Roaring Twenties or Great Depression with illustrations and maps.

- Come up with interview questions and assign the roles of interviewer and Prohibition-era bootlegger. Make a video of the interview with the bootlegger.

- Write and perform a short play about conditions in a Hooverville.

- Do a detailed comparison between any two of the men who were president in the 1920s and/or 1930s. Include ways they were alike and ways they were different.

- Make a scrapbook about the Roaring Twenties. Add captions for all pictures. You can download pictures from the Internet, photocopy them from books, or draw your own.

- Write articles for one page of a newspaper dated any time between 1920 and 1935.

- Write and illustrate a poem about the Roaring Twenties. Read your poem to the group.

- Make a model of a biplane and explain how it worked.

- Learn and demonstrate a dance popular in the Roaring Twenties, like the Charleston or the Lindy Hop. Teach others to do the dance.

- Write a detailed report about the conditions in your city or community during the Great Depression. Include copies of local newspaper articles.

- Create a journal that could have been written by someone between 1929 and 1935 describing everyday life and events. Include at least five entries for each year.

- Prepare and present a ten-minute speech either in favor of or against Prohibition.

Name: ____ Date: _____________________

Learn More About …

Learn more about one of the people listed below who had an impact on American history during the Roaring Twenties and/or the Great Depression Era. Use the Internet and other reference sources to write a three- to five-page report with illustrations.

Walt Disney

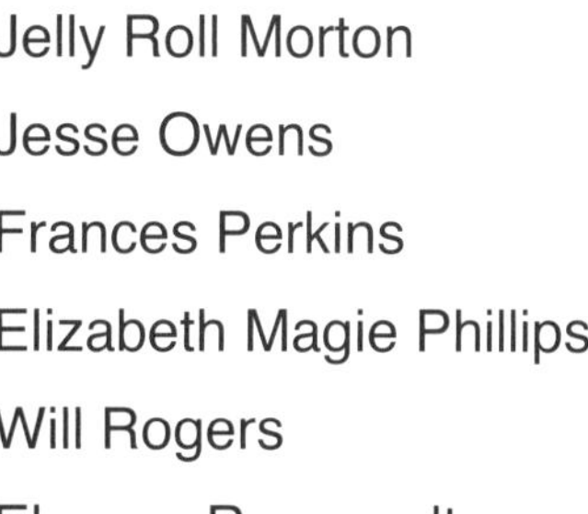

Isadora Duncan

Marian Anderson
Louis Armstrong
Pearl S. Buck
Richard Byrd
Al Capone
Charlie Chaplin
Calvin Coolidge
Douglas Corrigan
Charles Coughlin
Walt Disney
Isadora Duncan
Amelia Earhart
Duke Ellington
Edna Ferber
Henry Ford
George Gershwin
Benny Goodman
Woody Guthrie
Warren G. Harding
Ernest Hemingway
Herbert Hoover
Harry Houdini
Sinclair Lewis
Charles Lindbergh
Huey Long
Amy Lowell
Margaret Mead

Jelly Roll Morton
Jesse Owens
Frances Perkins
Elizabeth Magie Phillips
Will Rogers
Eleanor Roosevelt
Franklin D. Roosevelt
Nellie Tayloe Ross
Florence Sabin
Margaret Sanger
Upton Sinclair
Bessie Smith
Gertrude Stein
John Steinbeck
Francis Townsend
Rudolph Valentino

Amelia Earhart

Rudolph Valentino

Answer Keys

Women Finally Allowed to Vote (p. 7)
1. Wyoming in 1869
2. and 3. Answers will vary. See map.
4. With the exception of New York, none of the eastern or southern states had allowed full suffrage before the Nineteenth Amendment was passed. The states that did were all west of the Mississippi River.

Louis Armstrong: Master of Improvisation (p. 12)
1. Improvise: to make up something as you go along
2. Ensemble: a group, usually of musicians
3. "Hello, Dolly"
4. Satchmo; also Dippermouth, Satchelmouth, and Pops

Meet John Calvin Coolidge (p. 13)
1. and 2. Answers will vary.
3. July 4, 1872, in Plymouth Notch, Vermont
4. Silent Cal
5. Republican
6. Lawyer
7. "Keep Cool with Coolidge"

What Could You Buy for a Dollar? (p. 16)
1. 27
2. Yes; you would have enough left to go to three movies.
3. 20   4. 14   5. $1.00

Learning a New Language: Twenties' Slang (p. 17)
1. B   2. M   3. H   4. F   5. L   6. R
7. A   8. G   9. N   10. C   11. O   12. Q
13. E   14. P   15. D   16. K   17. I   18. J

Twenties Scavenger Hunt (p. 18)
1. The Green Bay Packers
2. Margaret Gorman of Washington, D.C.
3. Chicago Bears
4. balloon (inflatable) tires
5. a German shepherd dog
6. Nellie Tayloe Ross
7. The Harlem Globetrotters
8. *The Spirit of St. Louis*
9. 33 hours and 32 minutes
10. Alexander Fleming

Up, Up, and Away (p. 19)
1. O   2. F   3. F   4. O
5. F   6. O   7. F   8. O

Who's Who? (p. 20)
1. singer (opera)   2. dancer/actor
3. author   4. actor
5. pilot   6. boxer
7. film maker/artist/(voice) actor
8. pilot   9. (jazz) musician/composer
10. musician/composer   11. (jazz) musician
12. football player   13. actress
14. magician   15. golfer
16. boxer   17. anthropologist/author
18. (jazz) musician/composer
19. Olympic medal winner (track)
20. baseball player   21. (jazz) singer
22. author   23. tennis player
24. boxer
25. Olympic medal winner (swimmer)/actor

The Other Side of the Coin (p. 22)
All would be Then & Now except playing video games, watching television, and riding skateboards, which would be Now Only.

Review the Twenties (p. 24)
1. C   2. H   3. A   4. F   5. G   6. D
7. J   8. I   9. E   10. B   11. F   12. T
13. F   14. T   15. T   16. F   17. T   18. F
19. F   20. F

The Crash Heard Around the World (p. 26)
2. Depression: a time when prices are high and wages, low; often marked by periods of high unemployment

The 1930s and the Beginning of the Great Depression (p. 27)
1. Bankruptcy: broke; having no money; being unable to pay one's debts

Meet Young Franklin D. Roosevelt (p. 31)
1. James M. Cox

The Lame Duck Amendment (p. 34)
1. They wanted to decrease the time between the election and when the officials took office.
2. A "lame duck" was considered helpless or ineffective. Someone who had not been reelected was often helpless to get anything done in the time after the election until his term ended.
3. Answers will vary.
4. There must be a clear line of people who are qualified to take over the presidency so that the government can continue smoothly even in a crisis situation.

Math Facts (p. 35)
1. $24
2. $1,248
3. Answer will depend on current year.
4. 4,726 miles
5. 7 hours
6. $0.50 per hour
7. $169
8. $15
9. $360
10. 36%
11. 15,856,593
12. 17,064,426

What Happened When? (p. 38)
1. 1932 in Lake Placid, New York
2. *LIFE* and *Look*
3. *Snow White and the Seven Dwarfs*
4. Franklin D. Roosevelt   5. 1931
6. Half
7. Empire State Building
8. Cost rose from 2 cents to 3 cents
9. Frances Perkins   10. 13 million
11. 40 cents an hour   12. Twenty-First
13. 1935   14. electric typewriters
15. *Funnies on Parade*

New Deal Programs (p. 40)
2. The workers built roads and hiking trails, cleaned beaches, cleared camping sites, laid telephone lines, built fire observation towers, and planted trees. These projects benefitted the public.

An Alphabet Soup of New Deal Programs (p. 41)
1. Federal Deposit Insurance Corporation
2. Tennessee Valley Authority
3. Federal Emergency Relief Administration
4. Agricultural Adjustment Act
5. Home Owners' Loan Corporation
6. National Recovery Administration

Desperate Times, Desperate People, Desperate Actions (p. 42)
1. It got rid of the Association's surplus of apples, made apples available to the consumers, and gave the unemployed a source of income.

Major Projects of the Depression Era (p. 44)
1. a. 4   b. 5   c. 1   d. 7   e. 3   f. 2   g. 6

Let's Listen to the Radio (p. 45)
1. Music, news, weather, sports, advertisements, comedies, dramas
2. Television and the Internet
3. The actors had to look the part for their characters in television and movies.

Meet Eleanor Roosevelt (p. 46)
1. mother, maternal grandmother
2. nine
3. England
4. Franklin Roosevelt
5. My Day

6. Boulder (Hoover)
7. Lincoln Memorial
8. United Nations
9. Roosevelt
10. former U.S. President, Theodore Roosevelt

Thirties Scavenger Hunt (p. 49)
1. Kaw
2. Babe Ruth
3. Ronald Reagan
4. tax evasion
5. The "William Tell Overture"
6. Jay Silverheels
7. Gene Autry
8. Band leader
9. Arthur Jacob Arshawsky

The Social Security Act of 1935 (p. 50)
1. Unemployment Compensation
2. Old-Age Benefits (Social Security)

The Dust Bowl (p. 51)
1. Reservoir: a place to hold water for later use
2. Irrigation: a system used to carry water to where it is needed
3. Erosion: wearing away of soil due to wind or rain
4. Drought: period of little or no rain

Conditions Get Worse (p. 52)
1. Utah, Arizona, New Mexico, Colorado, Wyoming, Nebraska, Iowa, Missouri, Tennessee, Arkansas, and Louisiana
2. Wyoming, Nebraska, and Iowa
3. New Mexico, Texas, Oklahoma, and Kansas

A Cottage for Sale (p. 53)

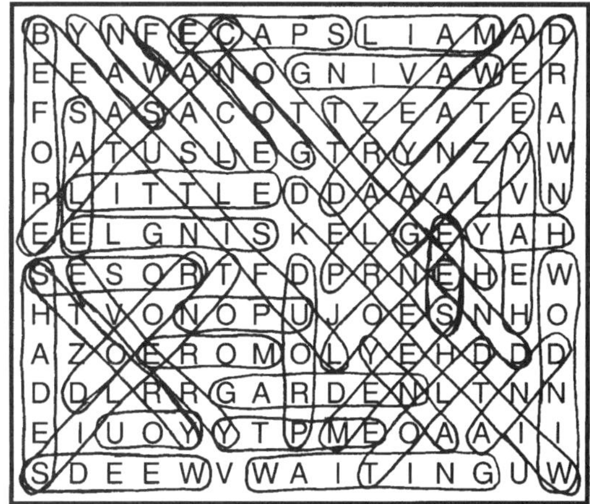

Review of the Thirties (p. 54)
1. D   2. G   3. E   4. F   5. H   6. B
7. C   8. A   9. F   10. T   11. F   12. F
13. T   14. F   15. F   16. T   17. F   18. T

Suggested Reading

The 1920s (American Popular Culture Through History) by Kathleen Drowne and Patrick Huber

The 1920s: The Scopes Monkey Trial by David B. McCoy

The 1930s (American Popular Culture Through History) by William H. Young

An Album of the Great Depression by William Loren Katz

Al Capone and Eliot Ness: Rivals During Prohibition by Lindsay Lowe

Calvin Coolidge by Zachary Kent

Calvin Coolidge: The American Presidents Series: The 30th President, 1923–1929 by David Greenberg

Children of the Dust Bowl: The True Story of the School at Weedpatch Camp by Jerry Stanley

Franklin D. Roosevelt by Alice Osinski

The Great Depression by David Downing

The Great Depression: A History from Beginning to End by Hourly History

Herbert Hoover by Susan Clinton

Herbert Hoover: The American Presidents Series: The 31st President, 1929–1933 by William Edward Leuchtenburg

A History of US: War, Peace, and All that Jazz: 1918–1945 by Joy Hakim

Life During the Great Depression by Dennis Nishi

The LIFE History of the United States: Volume 10, Boom & Bust 1917–32 and Volume 11, New Deal & War 1933–45 by Henry Graff & Time-Life

The Lindbergh Baby Kidnapping in American History by Judith Edwards

The Lindbergh Child: America's Hero and the Crime of the Century by Rick Geary

The Noble Experiment, 1919–1933 by James P. Barry

The Prohibition Era: Temperance in the United States by Louise Chipley Slavicek

Prohibition: The Rise and Fall of the Temperance Movement by Richard Worth

The Roaring Twenties by R. Conrad Stein

The Scopes Monkey Trial: A Headline Court Case by Freya Ottem Hanson

The Story of the Great Depression by R. Conrad Stein

The Story of the Teapot Dome Scandal by Jim Hardgrove

The Teapot Dome Scandal: A Headline Court Case by Jonathan L. Thorndike

The Teapot Dome Scandal: Corruption Rocks 1920s America by Barbara J. Davis

Ticket to the Twenties: A Time Traveler's Guide by Mary Blocksma

Timelines: 1920s by Gail B. Stewart

Timelines: 1930s by Gail B. Stewart

The Thirties: An Illustrated History in Colour 1930–1939 by R.J. Unstead

The Twenties: An Illustrated History in Colour 1919–1929 by R.J. Unstead

Warren G. Harding by Linda R. Wade

Warren G. Harding: The American Presidents Series: The 29th President, 1921–1923 by John W. Dean